STUDIES IN HISTORY, ECONOMICS, AND PUBLIC LAW

EDITED BY THE FACULTY OF POLITICAL SCIENCE
OF COLUMBIA UNIVERSITY

Number 277

NEGRO ILLEGITIMACY IN NEW YORK CITY

NEGRO ILLEGITIMACY IN NEW YORK CITY

BY

RUTH REED

AMS PRESS
NEW YORK

COLUMBIA UNIVERSITY
STUDIES IN THE
SOCIAL SCIENCES

277

The Series was formerly known as
Studies in History, Economics and Public Law

Reprinted with the permission of Columbia University Press
From the edition of 1926, New York
First AMS EDITION published 1968
Manufactured in the United States of America

Library of Congress Catalogue Card Number: 68-57577

AMS PRESS, INC.
NEW YORK, N.Y. 10003

To

MISS GRACE R. BOLEN

WITHOUT WHOSE HELP THE STUDY WOULD
NOT HAVE BEEN POSSIBLE

PREFACE

MANY people believe that individual and social difficulties of adjustment change in hue and tone when the color line is crossed. This belief is particularly marked when the situations considered are those centering about family life and the departures from the conventional forms of family life. There is a belief held by many social workers that illegitimacy among Negroes creates few social problems which are comparable in importance with those produced among white people by unconventional births. Facts do not exist by which the validity of such a belief can be tested because descriptions of the conditions which accompany illegitimacy among both Negro and white groups are so generally lacking. This study does not aim to settle the question of how illegitimacy among Negroes differs from illegitimacy among white people. The object is merely to present descriptive material with regard to some of the problems created by illegitimacy among a selected group of Negroes in New York City with the hope that such material may prove useful when comparable data for white groups shall be available.

The interest in making such a study grew out of a summer's work in social service at Sloane Hospital for Women where a considerable number of Negro unmarried mothers are given care. Grateful acknowledgment is made to Miss Grace R. Bolen of the social service department of the hospital, for permission to use the hospital records and for her aid in securing an opportunity to study the case records of other social agencies which have to do with Negro unmarried mothers and their infants.

RUTH REED.

AURORA, N. Y., MARCH, 1926.

7

TABLE OF CONTENTS

INTRODUCTION

CHAPTER I

SOCIETY AND THE UNMARRIED MOTHER

CHAPTER II

THE NEGRO UNMARRIED MOTHER IN NEW YORK CITY. HER BACKGROUND AND CHARACTERISTICS

CHAPTER III

THE SOCIAL AND ECONOMIC DIFFICULTIES OF NEGRO UNMARRIED MOTHERS

INTRODUCTION

FAMILY LIFE as a mother and child unit has always existed among human beings. Human mothers must, from the beginning of the species, have found it pleasurable to have their helpless young with them, and whatever be the nature of that vague and ill-defined force, the maternal instinct, there has always been some natural impulse which impelled the human mother to keep her child with her and to experience satisfaction in doing so. That the human father arrived at his place of sanctioned relationship to the original female and offspring unit by a route so in line with his natural proclivities seems doubtful, the more logical inference being that by many experiments and over many differing folkways he arrived at a place in the family group, the character of his relationship varying as greatly as the routes by which he had come.

Once the form which family relationships had assumed received the social sanction, then any deviation from the sanctioned form resulted in the disapproval of the group. Disapproval of deviations from accepted forms has varied in intensity with the nature of the sanctions given to the forms of family life. When particular patterns of family life have come to be associated with property rights or ideas of an emotional or religious nature, then any deviations from the accepted forms have been regarded as inimical to the interests of the group; the reaction of the group to the deviations has been emotional in tone and the punishment meted out ill-proportioned to the degree of social harm wrought. In cases where society has come to view its institutions in the light which has been thrown upon their origin and evolution some attempt has been made to view violations of its standards rationally and to apportion blame and censure in the same manner.

Illegitimacy or the birth of children outside of the sanctioned forms of family life has resulted in social problems which are similar in nature from one group to another; but the intensity of the problems created has varied with the customs, attitudes, and social conditions of the group. There are problems involving the adjustments of illegitimate parents, particularly mothers, to the conditions created for them by social disapproval of their conduct and situation; and there are problems of the adjustment of the offspring of these parents to the difficulties created for them by the bar sinister of their illegitimate birth. On the side of the parents there are personal and family relationships to be adjusted and social scorn and disapproval to be palliated or escaped; and all of these problems exist and are intensified in the case of the offspring. The question of the adjustment of the illegitimate child has probably received the greater share of society's attention because of the burden entailed by his support; and the difference between his environment and that of the child of legitimate birth is seen in the higher infant mortality rate, the higher juvenile delinquency rate, and the higher rate of crime among adults of illegitimate birth.[1] The difficulties which the mother has encountered and the adjustments which she has been able to make are registered to some extent in the quality of the environmental influences which have affected her child. Knowledge of the influences which have resulted in the creation of her difficulties and the adjustments which she has been able to make can be gained only from an analysis of those factors in her personal and environmental history which have been influential in producing her conduct and

[1] Mangold, *Children Born Out of Wedlock*, University of Missouri Studies, vol. iii, no. 3, p. 131.

the records of the adjustments which she has been able to make subsequent to the birth of her child.

Because of the prevalent belief that illegitimacy produces social complications among Negroes different in aspect from those produced among whites this study has been limited to a selected group of Negro women of New York City who are mothers of illegitimate children. An attempt has been made to analyze the relationship of society to unmarried mothers under varying conditions and at different periods of history; to see the nature and extent of the problem of illegitimacy among Negroes; and to ascertain those factors in the personal and environmental histories of this selected group of Negro unmarried mothers which have been influential in producing their delinquency, the nature of the situation created by their conduct, and the adjustments which they have been able to make to their changed situation. Whenever the nature and extent of our data have permitted comparisons have been made with the results of similar studies among white groups.

Research of this nature has been hindered by the taboos placed upon a phenomenon involving unsanctioned sex relations. Statistics obtainable from birth and death certificates while valuable for presenting an idea of the extent and distribution of the problem of illegitimacy are yet inadequate to present a complete picture of the social situation created. Knowledge of the circumstances leading up to the fact of unmarried motherhood among Negroes and of the manner in which the difficulties have been met in the lives of the individual variants from accepted forms is necessary to a complete understanding of the situation; and such information is difficult to obtain. The method of the personal interview conducted by a single investigator would have required the expenditure of much time and effort and would have possessed little value because the information secured could have received only very inadequate verification. Involved also was the difficulty of securing an adequate sample, a group which was representative of the total class of unmarried mothers considered.

The information found to be most easily available was contained in the case records of the various social and philanthropic agencies which have had dealings with the Negro unmarried mothers either in the matter of supplying them with financial aid or of furnishing guidance for them in making their adjustments to community life. The material contained in the case records was felt to be valuable because it was gathered by the social investigator with no other apparent purpose than to aid her in understanding and being of assistance to the case under consideration. Information which was felt to be necessary in most cases included a brief account of the subject's immediate situation and past history, her relationship to her family, their attitude toward her and her conduct, and their willingness or unwillingness to cooperate with her in making her plans for the future. In many cases the worker felt it necessary to interview the father of the child, and ascertain his attitude toward the girl to see whether a marriage could be arranged or whether legal steps were necessary to compel the father to support his child. Knowledge of the case's occupational history was needed also in order to guide the social worker in suggesting possible lines of employment for her in the future. The attitude of the former employer to the girl and her work was secured whenever possible; and, in securing a new situation it was important to find out the opinion of a possible employer toward the woman after the birth of her illegitimate child. The attitude of the unmarried mother toward her child, toward the social situation produced for her by having given birth to a child out of wedlock, and the adjustments which it was possible for her to make were also judged important in the worker's consideration of the case.

By comparison of the records for white unmarried mothers with the records kept for colored unmarried mothers it was found that the records for the colored group were much less complete both as to information contained and evidence of effort and attention given to the cases than those for the white group. Case workers explain this by the greater difficulty of keeping in touch with the colored women, less willingness on their part to coöperate in the plans suggested by the agency, their apparent lack of concern for their own welfare, and their frequent unwillingness to bring suit against the father of the child in order to compel him to contribute to the child's support. Work with colored unmarried mothers was therefore felt to be particularly difficult not only because of the disproportionate numbers in which they come to the attention of the agencies but also because of the greater difficulties in securing their active coöperation.

The agencies whose records were examined make no discrimination on the grounds of race or color and the white workers employed appeared to be remarkably free from race prejudice. However, it seems possible that the sense of group and race consciousness which enters into and gives quality to all of our personal relationships had operated to raise barriers which had rendered difficult a frank relationship between white worker and colored case. Colored social workers, in cases where they had been employed by the agencies, had apparently found it possible to secure information regarding personal and family history much more easily and adequately and had thus been able to proceed further in their guidance of conduct.

Records for both white and colored cases were often lacking in information which might have been of value to the investigator in understanding the case's conduct and history. There were evidences that the workers' inquiry had often extended further than the records indicated, and that in the press of other duties the workers, though in possession of other information, had failed to record it. Often, too, impressions of the case's attitude and emotional state which had been important factors in determining the advice given were not included in the records. In some cases it was possible to supplement the information given in a record by an interview with the worker who had had charge of the case. Of more importance than the failure of the workers to record the information which they had in hand was the fact that, from the very nature of their situation, they became so concerned with the immediate solution of the difficulties presented that adequate time was not given to the investigation and recording of factors in the case's environment which might have operated as causative influences and knowledge of which might have been useful in the solution of the difficulties presented.

Access was had to the records of the State Charities Aid Association, the Church Mission of Help, the Association for Improving the Condition of the Poor, Sloane Hospital for Women, the Department of Public Welfare, and the Katy Ferguson Home. After sample records from the several agencies had been read, it was determined to what extent the material contained in the records would lend itself to tabulation. A plan for tabulation was then devised, and the data contained in the 500 selected records was grouped under the categories of information included in the schedule. The results were then assembled and presented in tabular form. Comparisons were made with previous studies when possible. It was found that the material dealing with the personal and environmental history of the mothers of illegitimate children was more abundant than that dealing with the history of their children because of the difficulty of the agencies in keeping in touch with their cases for any considerable period of time after the birth of the child.

Since available figures from the Department of Health do not permit of enlightening comparisons with illegitimacy rates of other racial groups of the population of the City of New York, no attempt was made to limit the selection of cases to a given year and the sole basis of selection was that of the adequacy of the information contained in the records. Most of the cases have been selected from those coming to the attention of the agencies during the years 1922-1923 but there has been no hesitation in using records covering a longer period when completeness of information and quality of descriptive material made the record valuable for the purpose of the study. The result has been, therefore, the examination of a group of records selected on no other basis than the adequacy of the information contained in them. To test the validity of our sample, data contained in the records of the same agency have been classified by year periods with results closely comparable with the results obtained when data for the entire sample were classified.

The difficulties of our manner of investigation were recognized when an attempt was made to classify the data contained in the records. The information which we found in the records while not gathered with a view to uniformity or to later classification, has yet been sufficiently uniform in type to warrant tabulation and description of certain features as common to the group. The nature of the information contained in the case histories varied greatly from one agency to another, but certain essential facts were contained in all; the greatest difficulties being that the information was often stated in ambiguous terms, or for particular categories of our classification was altogether missing. Interviews with workers, however, clarified many of the difficulties and were of aid in getting the material in a form in which comparisons were possible.

It is difficult to say whether the Negro unmarried mothers coming to the attention of social agencies in New York constitute a representative sample of the total group of Negro unmarried mothers in the City. There is at once left out of account a group who might either be so capable in the adjustment of their own affairs or so successful in concealing the fact of unmarried motherhood that they would have no occasion to consult these agencies; and another group who either would not know of the existence or the availability of these agencies or whose standards are such that they would not be sensitive to any difficulties or discomforts arising from their situation. Nevertheless, those who do come to the attention of the agencies may be assumed to be representative of those who constitute a direct cost to the community either because of the financial aid which must be granted them or because of the time and energy which must be expended by social workers in aiding them to make adjustments in home or occupation; and, as such, they constitute a problem worthy of consideration by the sociologist.

As to the conclusions drawn from the study, they can be no broader than for the group studied. It has been assumed that the selected group is representative of the type of cases coming to the attention of social agencies in the City of New York, yet it must be borne in mind that there are many cases of illegitimacy that are not discovered or dealt with by social agencies at all, and that of those who do come to the attention of these agencies the great number are from the lower economic groups, in which a majority of the Negro women are found. Great caution, therefore, will have to be used in extending conclusions farther than this group of Negro women of the lower economic groups who have come to the attention of social agencies in the locality studied.

CHAPTER I

Society and the Unmarried Mother

Throughout civilized time society has attempted to safeguard the conditions under which children shall be born by recognition of some form of the institution of marriage as necessary for the maintenance of the group and the upbringing of children. A study of the social organization of primitive peoples likewise reveals the family as an omnipresent social unit. Morgan's [1] hypothesis of the family as a relatively late product of social evolution preceded by a long period of promiscuity and group marriage has not stood the scrutiny of modern research and it is now admitted that in every community of which we have record there has existed some form of family life in which the husband and wife and immature children constitute a unit apart from the remaider of the community.[2]

The forms of marriage which have received social sanction have varied from one group to another and within the same group at different periods of its history, but conformity to the sanctioned modes has been at all times the criterion for fixing the place of the mother and her child within the group. Westermarck's generalization [3] that " marriage is a more or less durable connection between made and female lasting beyond the mere act of propagation and until after the birth of the offspring " might seem to indicate that the

---

[1] Morgan, *Ancient Society* (New York, 1877), p. 383 *et seq.*
[2] Lowie, *Primitive Society* (New York, 1920), p. 66.
[3] Westermarck, *History of Human Marriage* (New York, 1901), ch. i.

biological parentage of the child serves as the basis for the fixing of his conventional guardians. But if, as Hartland maintains,[1] the fact of paternity was established relatively late in the development of society, then the status of the mother and her child under the earlier conditions must have been determined by the customs and standards of the group without reference to the natural father of the child. Among the Todas,[2] paternity as a social fact is established by a conventional rite without reference to the biological paternity of the child. According to tribal usage a woman may become the wife of several men who may all live in different villages. If such is the case, the woman lives with each of her husbands in turn, passing from one village to another in the performance of her marital duties. If she becomes pregnant, that one of her husbands who first performs a prescribed ceremony with a bow and arrow is recognized as the father of her child and of any children that may be born subsequently until another of the husbands performs the necessary ceremony. Among certain other tribes of India, East Africa and North America, the father, who is selected by a conventional rite, performs all the duties of progenitor for the children declared to be his by social sanction. Neglect on the part of the mothers among these tribes to perform certain ceremonials preceding the birth of the child is followed by severe penalties for them and their offspring.[3]

Under modern conditions where the biological paternity of the child is considered of first importance and the marriage institution itself is regarded as a device for insuring the establishment of paternity, compliance with the socially approved form of the institution is the basis for the group sanction of motherhood; and the status of the woman giving

[1] Hartland, *Primitive Paternity* (London, 1909), vol. i, ch. iv.

[2] Lowie, *op. cit.*, p. 47.

[3] Lowie, *op. cit.*, p. 45.

birth to a child out of wedlock is, of necessity, different from that of the mother who has complied with the dictates of the group. It is assumed that in complying with the marriage regulations provision is made for the care of children and society makes no formal provision for the existence or for the care of a mother and her child outside of the sanctioned forms. The English common law, and in this respect the American common law also, designates the illegitimate child as *filius nullius,* the child of nobody, without name, without kin, and without claim on any for support.[1] The child is regarded as the symbol of the defiance of society's mandates, his existence as an affront to the group's most cherished traditions. On him as the evidence of his parents' sinning is visited the displeasure of the group expressed in lack of social esteem, in social scorn and disapproval, and in restrictions placed upon action and opportunity which lessen materially his chances of survival.

The type of union approved within any given group is more easily maintained because it comes to be associated with property and inheritance rights, and when to these there is added a strong religious sentiment as a means of protecting the institution, then the social stigma attached to any departure from the standard becomes very great. Extramarital unions are regarded as inimical to the interests of the group and as subversive of standards around which have come to be centered strong emotions, social and religious in nature. While the child is usually the chief sufferer from society's displeasure, whenever the parents have been taken into account the direct social penalties have fallen more heavily upon the mother than upon the father, because she has been the more obvious parent; and the mother has been subjected to various penalties and curtailments of privilege

---

[1] Freund, *Illegitimacy Laws of the United States and Certain Foreign Countries,* Federal Children's Bureau (Washington, 1919), p. 9.

as a result of her unsocial conduct. Among the Kabyles an unmarried woman becoming pregnant is sentenced to death and her lover suffers a heavy fine.[1] Among the ancient Hebrews the woman under such circumstances was legally required to suffer the death penalty unless it could be proved that she resented the advances of the man who was the father of her child.[2] At the beginning of the Christian era marriage was brought under the supervision of the Church and, in the thirteenth century, was made one of the holy sacraments. Punishment for violation of its sacredness, therefore, rested in the hands of the Church.[3] Throughout the Middle Ages, a frequent punishment for unmarried motherhood was public penance and open confession before the congregation; but this resulted in such an alarming prevalence of infanticide that the severity of the punishment had to be somewhat relaxed and asylums provided for the reception of infants.[4] As late as 1752 Frederick the Great, wrote to Voltaire that of the executions taking place in Prussia the most of them were " of girls who had killed their infants and a much lesser number of other murderers and a few highwaymen." [5] Punishment of unmarried mothers during the early colonial days in America was by open confession in the church, imprisonment in the stocks, or some other form of punishment involving public humiliation and social ostracism.[6] In Connecticut in 1645 the General Court ordered the father and the mother of such a child to be whipped, and in 1699 it was ordered that " for con-

---

[1] Parsons, *The Family* (New York, 1906), p. 131.

[2] *Ibid.*, p. 133.

[3] Howard, *History of Matrimonial Institutions* (Chicago, 1904), vol. i, p. 296 *et seq.*

[4] Werner, *The Unmarried Mother in German Literature* (New York, 1917), p. 86 *et seq.*

[5] *Ibid.*, p. 89.

[6] Freund, *op. cit.*, p. 18.

cealing the death of a child who, if born alive, would have been a bastard the mother was to suffer as in the case of murder unless she could prove by at least one witness that the child was born dead." [1]

Later years have seen no form of positive punishment of unmarried motherhood by the civil authorities, but disabilities have been imposed by means of discriminations against such mothers in legislation providing for mothers' pensions.[2] In 39 of the United States that have enacted mothers' pension laws only two states, Michigan and Nebraska, make provision for the unmarried mother and one other state, Wisconsin, makes provision for a " mother without a husband ".[3] Twenty-nine of the states extend the benefits only to mothers of legitimate children, while the remaining make such specification as to character, standing in the community, and good conduct as may be held to exclude the unmarried mother.[4] A few of the states extend the benefits of workmen's compensation to illegitimate children if they are being supported by the father at the time of the accident.[5] As to discriminations practiced by private welfare agencies less complete data exist, but Dr. Carol Aronovici in a study of social agencies in Philadelphia found that of the 32 maternity hospitals, 5 refused to take unmarried mothers and 5 would take them only in cases of emergency. Out of a total of 61 agencies that were non-sectarian 8 discriminated against unmarried mothers and their children, while in the agencies connected with religious institutions, of which there were 20, twelve discriminated against such mothers and their chil-

---

[1] *Ibid.*, p. 29.

[2] Federal Children's Bureau, *Illegitimacy as a Child Welfare Problem* (Washington, 1920), vol. ii, p. 39.

[3] *Illegitimacy as a Child Welfare Problem, op. cit.*, vol. i, p. 39.

[4] *Ibid.*, p. 39.

[5] *Ibid.*, p. 38.

dren. In other words, the amount of discrimination on the part of sectarian agencies was 4½ times greater than it would have been if judged by the standard of the non-sectarian institutions.[1]

Aside from these types of discrimination that can be measured, unmarried mothers suffer most perhaps from the forms of social disapproval that express themselves in slights, loss of social position and esteem, and exclusion from accustomed lines of employment. A woman who is known to have given birth to a child out of wedlock is " ruined ", " fallen ", or " gone astray ". In rural districts or in conservative communities, where standards are rigidly adhered to, her family shares in her disgrace; and ostracism at the hands of the community may extend even to business relations. Designations applied to institutions where unmarried mothers from the lower economic groups are received are further indications of society's attitude. These are known as " homes of refuge ", " rescue homes ", " homes of the good shepherd", "heart's ease", and "doors of hope". The assumption regarding the spiritual havoc which these women are supposed to have suffered as a result of their experiences is shown by the program of these institutions, which is to " rescue ", to " reform " and to " rehabilitate " the inmates. They are also to be aided in " regaining their self-respect "; " morale " is to be built up; and at the completion of the process the woman is to be " restored " to a place of usefulness in the community. Recently the policy of some social agencies has been to encourage the unmarried mother to keep her child with her instead of leaving it in an institution or placing it with an agency for adoption upon returning to the community. A woman without a wedding ring working with a child in domestic service or in such positions as the agencies are able to find, is subject

[1] Aronovici, *Unpublished Study of Illegitimacy in Philadelphia.*

to repeated insults at the hands of men whom she meets from day to day, hence some of the institutions now permit " rehabilitated " girls to return to community life with a wedding ring as an additional source of protection.

Unmarried mothers of means escape the necessity for this method of protection. Advertisements of maternity homes evidently designed to meet the needs of this class of women are " private", " strictly confidential ", and " safe". "Homes provided for infants " and " adoption arranged for " are additional attractions offered in states where legal regulations do not forbid.

The well-known unreliability of statistics concerning illegitimacy is another indication of the tendency to concealment of irregular relations in order to escape social stigma. A study of case records of social agencies in Boston by the Federal Children's Bureau [1] added one-eighth to the number of illegitimate births registered as such in the city and a study of the death certificates of children under one year of age revealed further the incompleteness of registration. In some states both parents of an illegitimate child are protected by law from having their identity revealed on the birth certificate. In the District of Columbia the law states " that it shall in no case be necessary for any physician, midwife or other person to report fact or facts whereby the identity of the father or mother of the child born shall be disclosed." [2] In North Carolina and Illinois there is a similar provision.[3] Other states safeguard only the identity of the father. In six states the law forbids the entry of the name of the father on the birth certificate of an illegitimate child, while in Georgia, Massachusetts, Minnesota, and New York the father's name may be entered only by his consent.[4] The

---

[1] *Illegitimacy as a Child Welfare Problem, op. cit.,* vol. ii, p. 87.

[2] *Ibid.,* vol. i, p. 19.

[3] *Ibid.,* p. 19.

[4] *Ibid.,* p. 20.

recommendations of the United States Bureau of the Census provide that the birth certificate shall state whether the child is legitimate or illegitimate, the full name of the father, and the maiden name of the mother.[1] The registration laws of only twenty states contain these provisions.[2]

The duty of the support of the child was early imposed upon the mother and not until recent years has cognizance been taken of the existence of the father to compel him to contribute to its support. The Napoleonic code which was, until recently, the law in France and Italy forbids inquiry into the paternity of the child of an unmarried mother.[3] In England the common law declares the illegitimate child to be *filius nullius,* but in certain police measures beginning with the Poor Law Amendment of 1834 the mother is to be held responsible for its support; and by subsequent legislation the father is to be compelled to contribute.[4] In the United States the relation of the mother to her illegitimate child is the same as her relation to her legitimate child, while in only one state, Minnesota, is the father held to the same degree of responsibility.[5] In Georgia it is declared that the mother is the only recognized parent of an illegitimate child, though the father may be compelled to contribute to the support of the child.[6]

While early measures taken by the state regarding the protection of the unmarried mother and her child grew out of the poor-law legislation and had for their object the protection of the state from the burden of the dependency of the child, the tendency of later legislation has been to recog-

[1] *Ibid.,* p. 21.

[2] *Ibid.,* p. 21.

[3] Freund, *op. cit.,* p. 9.

[4] *Ibid.,* p. 9.

[5] *Illegitimacy as a Child Welfare Problem,* vol. i, p. 42.

[6] Freund, p. 18.

nize the responsibility of the state to secure adequate care by compelling support by the father or by making provision for the granting of aid directly by the state. This new trend in legislation has probably been due to the recognition that illegitimacy rates for certain districts and for whole countries have remained uniform over long periods of time and the existence of the unmarried mother and her child has been seen as a persistent fact which non-recognition on the part of the state has done nothing to eliminate. The most advanced legislation looking to the provision for such mothers and their children has been enacted in Norway, where the state has accepted the responsibility for the protection of unmarried mothers and their infants and has set in motion the machinery for the purpose. If support cannot be secured from the father the state supplies the assistance. Particular attention is given to securing proper care for the mother and the state itself takes the initiative in establishing paternity.[1] Both parents are held to the same degree of responsibility for the care of the illegitimate child as for the legitimate child, and children born out of wedlock have the same right to their father's name and the same inheritance rights as those born in wedlock. Germany also has inaugurated a system of guardianship under which a public official is appointed to act as guardian for the illegitimate child and to aid and advise the mother in every way possible as to legal procedures necessary for securing support for her child. Paternity in the majority of cases is established and support is secured from the father of the child.[2] American legislation has been more conservative, but during the past decade there has been a marked change in social emphasis and the tendency to make conventional guardianship conform to biological parentage is evident. The Minnesota law

---

[1] *Illegitimacy as a Child Welfare Problem, op. cit.*, vol. i, p. 29.

[2] Freund, *op. cit.*, p. 249.

of 1917 declares that " the child's interest is in all cases paramount ", and it is furthermore declared to be the duty of the state to " safeguard the interest of illegitimate children and secure for them the nearest possible approximation to the care, support, and education they would be entitled to receive if born in lawful marriage." [1]   An attempt to remove the stigma attached to illegitimate birth is evident in the North Dakota law of 1917, which declares that every child is the " legitimate child " of its natural parents and should be entitled to support and education to the same extent as if born in lawful wedlock, and to the right to inherit from both parents and their kindred. [2]

The stigma attached to the mother as the natural custodian of the illegitimate child inhibits the functioning of her maternal impulses and results in a lack of interest in the welfare of the child.   This lack of interest in the child's survival together with the difficulties encountered in his support create an environment which is unfavorable from the outset, and the results of this are reflected in the high death rate of illegitimate infants.   The census does not furnish sufficient data to admit of comparisons of death rates for legitimate and illegitimate children, but a study by the Federal Children's Bureau shows that while the death rate among the children of legitimate birth in Boston in 1914 was 95 per 1000 for children under one year of age, the death rate per 1000 of those of illegitimate birth was 281, or three times as great for illegitimate as for legitimate infants. [3]   In Baltimore the white children of legitimate birth under one year of age died at a rate of 95.3 per 1000 while the mortality rate for the infants of illegitimate birth was 315.5 per 1000 or

[1] Laws ch. 210, Amending General Statutes 1913, section 3225.
[2] *Illegitimacy as a Child Welfare Problem, op. cit.,* vol. i, p. 38.
[3] *Illegitimacy as a Child Welfare Problem, op. cit.,* vol. ii, p. 88.

3.3 times as great.[1] Study of the causes of death show that
a large proportion of them are due to gastric and intestinal
diseases, which may be due to faulty feeding consequent upon
the early separation of mother and child. That separation of
mother and child as well as the attitude of the mother toward
her illegitimate child may be a factor in the death rate of
illegitimate children is shown by Leffingwell's study of the
reports of coroners' inquests held upon illegitimate children
under one year of age in England and Wales for a period
of six years. From these he found that illegitimate children
are four times as liable to " accidents " resulting in death
as are children of legitimate birth.[2]

There can be little doubt that to some extent at least this
higher mortality rate of infants is due to the more or less
conscious resentment on the part of the unmarried mothers
at the difficult economic and social position in which they
find themselves. And they are resentful — these women
trapped by their instincts and their ignorance into such a
situation. True it is that some, the dull or feebleminded or
unthinking ones, accept with humility what they regard as
the consequences of their " sins ", but often there is manifested an attitude of resentment, a disposition to fight back,
to get even. This is less seldom manifested by an unmarried mother as a feeling of resentment or bitterness against
the father of her child than a vague sullen resentment against
her situation in general, the hard condition of her lot.
Angry sullen looks and a stubborn refusal to coöperate with
the agencies seeking to find a situation for her with her
child are the usual indications of pent-up emotions; but
occasionally one of these girls becomes articulate and with
flashing eyes hurls back her defiance. These outbursts are

---

[1] *United States Children's Bureau, Infant Mortality in Baltimore*
(Washington, 1921), p. 67.

[2] Leffingwell, *Illegitimacy* (New York, 1892), p. 72.

more likely to occur when the claims of her child upon her are being urged. "Keep my child this way? Never! Claims on me, we'll see!"

Occasionally this attitude changes after longer association with the child. Bain [1] urges that maternal love arises from the pleasure of physical contact between female and off-spring, and certain it is that an unmarried mother is much more likely to be desirous of having her child with her permanently if she can be persuaded to nurse it during the first few weeks of its life. Occasionally, however, the attitude of indifference or dislike toward the child persists and the mother steadfastly refuses to have the child near her or accept any responsibility for its existence. G. Bernard Shaw has pointed out that children are to some extent necessarily and unavoidably a nuisance to grown-up persons—with their undisciplined and impulsive energy and their unlimited capacity for disturbing the comfort and tranquility of adult life — a menace from which even the most devoted parent must at times wish that he could free himself. With the burden of parenthood increased a thousandfold by the stigma attached to unconventional motherhood the desire and effort on the part of the unmarried mother to rid herself of her burden is not surprising. In the past when the strain upon her powers of endurance was pushed too far and there was no means of escape, then infanticide was widely prevalent, but under modern conditions the road to freedom is through concealment by separation from the child.

In making comparisons between the number of unmarried mothers in different communities something of the significance of illegitimacy statistics should be known before any deductions are drawn as to general social conditions. From records of illegitimate births there can be secured an estimate of the number of unmarried women who have be-

---

[1] Bain, *The Senses and the Intellect* (New York, 1888), p. 168.

come mothers during the year for which the rate was calculated. The figure usually includes mothers who have entered into marriages which have proved to be illegal or types of marriage which have no sanction in the law. The definition of the term illegitimacy, the manner of the collection of the statistics and the accuracy with which the records are kept may account for seemingly significant differences between groups. In Russia,[1] until recently, statistics concerning illegitimate births were secured from records of the church; in Germany [2] the collection of vital statistics was considered an important function of the state; while in the United States laws concerning the registration of births differ from state to state in such a manner as to make comparisons difficult.[3]

Even when statistics are accurate the number of unmarried mothers cannot be taken as an index of the prevalence of extra-marital sex relations in the group. Nixon in his study of Australian statistics points out that the illegitimacy rate would be almost doubled if the number of children born within the first six months after marriage were taken into consideration.[4] Nor do illegitimacy statistics take account of the irregular sex relations of women who have had the knowledge and foresight to prevent conception, or of women who resort to physicians for abortion when pregnancy results. On the contrary, unmarried motherhood in the United States is more often a result of youth, inexperience, ignorance, and amentia than of sophistication and experience in wrong-doing. Until society perfects and sanctions methods for complete birth control, with information concerning the

[1] *Illegitimacy as a Child Welfare Problem, op. cit.,* vol. i, p. 10.

[2] *Ibid.,* p. 11.

[3] *Ibid.,* p. 19.

[4] Nixon, " Some Factors Associated with the Illegitimate Birth Rate," *loc. cit., Journal of the Royal Statistical Society,* vol. 77, July, 1914.

methods accessible to all, the penalties inflicted upon unmarried motherhood are penalties inflicted upon youthful inexperience, ignorance, and feeblemindedness rather than penalties upon extra-marital sex relations. Opponents of measures looking toward the amelioration of the condition of the unmarried mother are prone to overlook this fact and urge that such measures would have the effect of increasing the prevalence of illegitimacy with danger to the ideal of the monogamous home. Popenoe urges that all such measures " which have for their object the endeavor to make illegitimate motherhood pleasanter and more respectable and to give to illegitimate children a better start in life must be looked upon with suspicion if not with actual disfavor." [1] Bingham [2] finds that where unmarried motherhood occurs among adolescent girls the circumstance can be attributed to environmental conditions of such a nature that there was no inhibiting prejudice regarding extra-marital pregnancies; to mental defect, or to ignorance on the part of the girl as to measures necessary to prevent conception or to the possibility of securing an abortion; to a deliberate desire on the part of the girl to court pregnancy as a means of forcing unwilling parents to consent to a marriage or as a means of forcing a procrastinating lover to make good his promises; to a genuine longing for children where marriage was impossible; or to conscientious scruples which prevent attempts to end pregnancy.

Changes in the legal definition of marriage may cause a sudden rise or fall in the illegitimacy rate without any corresponding change in social conditions. In a study of illegitimacy in Bulgaria, Townley Fullam [3] points out that the

---

[1] Popenoe, *loc. cit., Journal of Social Hygiene*, December, 1923.

[2] Bingham, *Determinants of Sex Delinquency in Adolescent Girls* (New York, 1923), p. 36 *et seq.*

[3] C. Townley Fullam, " Moral and Social Aspects of Illegitimacy in Hungary," *loc. cit., Forum*, vol. 50, pp. 618-650.

countries of Europe in her illegitimacy rate. She had until 1868 a statute forbidding marriage on the part of young men until they had secured a competence which was beyond the ability of large numbers of young men to secure by the time that they had reached a marriageable age.[1] Unlicensed unions under such conditions were frequent, but the unmarried mothers under these circumstances suffered little from social disapproval and their status was, in most circumstances, as favorable as that of the married women who were similarly situated economically. Changes in the marriage law resulted in a marked decrease in the illegitimacy rates within a single decade. Nixon,[2] in his study of Australian statistics, found a high degree of correlation between the number of illegitimate births and the number of unmarried men of marriageable age in the community: and similar studies of European countries where young men are required to serve in the army for a period of time before marriage bear out his conclusions.

Attempts to explain illegitimacy in terms of race have broken down under the scrutiny of comparative figures for members of the same race living in different countries or in the same country under different economic and social conditions. Caucasian Vienna and Austria have very high illegitimacy rates while the rates for Ireland and England are relatively low. South American countries, settled largely by peoples of Latin origin, have excessively high rates, but the rates in Italy and Spain, while relatively high, are yet lower than the rates in Denmark and Sweden.[3] Rates among the Negroes are invariably higher than the corresponding rates for the whites in the same communities, yet their rate varies with the rate for the whites and can be explained in terms

---

[1] Ryan, "Illegitimacy," *loc. cit., Catholic Encyclopaedia.*

[2] Nixon, *loc. cit., passim.*

[3] Ingram, "Illegitimacy," *loc. cit., International Encyclopaedia.*

of historical conditions and present social surroundings without reference to the factor of race.

Similar attempts to explain illegitimacy rates in terms of religious differences have not been successful when the inclusive terms of Protestantism and Catholicism have been used.[1]   Catholic Ireland has a very low illegitimacy rate and Catholic Austria a very high one, while the countries predominantly Protestant have rates showing as wide a range of variation.   However, a correlation would hardly be expected unless some categories could be devised to show the hold that religion has upon the lives of the people.

Climate has also been suggested as a factor influencing illegitimacy rates.   People of Southern climates are held to be more ardent in temperament and hence more inclined to disregard measures laying any restraint upon strong natural impulses; while people of Northern climates are considered to be more restrained in conduct because of the discipline which has to be inculcated in order to enable them to cope with the forces of nature.   This view has found strong support among those who believe in climate as the predominant factor in shaping the social life of peoples, but illegitimacy rates do not sustain the hypothesis.   The rate for Scotland is much higher than the rate for England, while the rates for Denmark and Sweden are higher than the rates for Spain and Italy.   On the other hand, the rate for Norway is relatively lower than the rate for Denmark and Sweden; and the rate for the German Empire is lower than the rate for Austria on the South.[2]

The presence of a large number of surplus women of marriageable age in the population is usually accompanied by a high illegitimacy rate unless offset by other conditions.[3]

[1] Mangold, *op. cit.*, p. 71.

[2] Ingram, *loc. cit.*, *passim.*

[3] Mangold, *op. cit.*, p. 75.

been so employed.[1] This condition has been found to prevail in other American cities where studies have been made of the histories of unmarried mothers. A corresponding study of Australian statistics indicates that the servant class contributes about 55 per cent of the illegitimate children while constituting only about 35 per cent of the total number of women in gainful occupations.[2]

No general conclusions can be drawn as to the age of mothers of illegitimate children since the average age for women of this group varies greatly from one country to another. In Scandinavia the greatest number of such women are between the ages of twenty-five and thirty-five, and even after forty the number is greater than for the age groups under twenty.[3]

The following shows the number of illegitimate births (including Negro but excluding stillbirths) per 1000 total births according to age of mother in the United States:[4]

TABLE No. I

ILLEGITIMATE BIRTHS PER 1000 BIRTHS IN THE REGISTRATION AREA OF THE
UNITED STATES 1920 BY AGE OF MOTHERS

10–14 years	668.6
15–19 "	113.2
20–24 "	25.7
25–29 "	8.9
30–34 "	6.1
35–39 "	6.7
40–44 "	6.0

Statistics for the German cities show that the greater incidence of illegitimacy is in the age groups after 20 and that the falling off of the numbers in the later age groups

[1] *Illegitimacy as a Child Welfare Problem, op. cit.,* vol. ii, p. 121.

[2] Nixon, *loc. cit., passim.*

[3] Leffingwell, *op. cit.,* p. 67.

[4] In the registration area excluding California and Massachusetts, *Birth Statistics 1920,* p. 25, Bureau of the Census, Washington, D. C.

is very slow.[1] Studies in Philadelphia and Cincinnati show that the Negro unmarried mothers are as a rule younger than the white unmarried mothers of the same community.[2] It is difficult to explain the differences in the average age of the unmarried mothers of the various groups for which statistics as to age are available. Ross [3] points out that a larger proportion of men and women in the United States are married than in any European countries except Bulgaria, Hungary, Servia, and Russia. We therefore have fewer women unmarried during the later years of the childbearing period and our illegitimacy rates for these age groups are lowered. In European countries where marriage rates are lower the temptation to irregular relations would be much greater—especially in the case of the older women whose hopes of marriage have been lessened with increasing age. Customs in certain European countries with regard to the chaperonage of young girls and the care with which they are guarded by their parents would operate to lower illegitimacy rates in the years before parental vigilance is lessened. Negro girls in this country are employed at an earlier age than are white girls, and this lessening of the home influences during the early years might explain in part the higher illegitimacy rates among young Negro girls. Not only are Negro girls employed at an earlier age but they are employed in greater numbers in the group of occupations in which the illegitimacy rate is higher in all countries, i. e. in domestic and personal service.[4] This combination of unfavorable circumstances for the young Negro girls raises considerably the illegitimacy rate in the lower age groups.

[1] Mangold, op. cit., p. 60.

[2] Aronovici, op. cit., passim; Trounstine, Illegitimacy in Cincinnati (Cincinnati, 1915), passim.

[3] Ross, Principles of Sociology (New York, 1920), p. 11 et seq.

[4] United States Bureau of the Census, 1920.

American studies reveal the fact that a very large number of the unmarried mothers come from homes where family relations are not normal but where desertion, divorce, step-parenthood, or the widowhood of the parents produced undesirable home relations for the girls. While no figures exist which make possible comparisons of home conditions of unmarried mothers with those of the general population, the frequency with which the conjugal condition of the parents of the unmarried mother is irregular seems to warrant the assumption that family irregularities occur much more frequently in the homes of the unmarried mothers than in the homes of the population at large. Of the 840 unmarried mothers whose histories were secured in the study in Boston, 261 or 31 per cent came from homes where one or both of the parents were missing. In the 18 to 20-year-old group 36 per cent were living away from home at the place of their employment previous to the birth of the first child.[1] Dr. Carol Aronovici mentions that of the girls studied at Sleighton Farms 67.24 per cent of the white girls and about 86.49 per cent of the colored girls came from homes where one or both of the parents were missing.[2] In addition to abnormalities in conjugal condition of the parents, the homes of the girls made a poor showing with respect to such matters as cleanliness and order, though data for the general population with regard to these matters are so generally lacking that comparisons cannot be made to determine whether these unfavorable conditions occur within the homes of the unmarried mothers with greater frequency than in the total economic group of which they are only a part. It must also be considered that in studying the population of an institution the occurrence of a broken home was probably one of

---

[1] *Illegitimacy as a Child Welfare Problem, op. cit.*, vol. ii, p. 120.

[2] Aronovici, *Unmarried Girls with Sex Experience* (Philadelphia, 1915), *passim.*

the causes for commitment to an institution and generalizations regarding the whole group of unmarried mothers cannot be drawn from facts gained from a group so highly selected.

As to the mentality of this group of women, evidence exists to prove that there is a disproportionate number of dull or feebleminded individuals in the group. Jean Weidsenall concludes from the results of two sets of tests that she gave to the unmarried mothers of the Cincinnati General Hospital that no more than 20 per cent of the members of this group should be considered of normal mentality; but of an unselected group of married mothers of the same economic standing about 50 per cent could be considered of normal intelligence. She concludes that from 40 to 45 per cent of the unmarried mothers are without question of such low-grade mentality that " life under institutional conditions would be the only happy one for themselves and the most economical and safe one for society." Results from other studies confirm these conclusions but the early enthusiasm over the Intelligence Quotient as a diagnostic index has somewhat subsided and it is now being recognized that the temperament, habits, and desires of the individual are equally as influential as is intelligence in determining conduct.[1] Study at Sleighton Farms of the girls under 21 who were classed as immoral, shows that there was in this group no relation between frequency of immorality and feeblemindedness and that the girls who had a record of immorality had as a rule better occupational records on leaving the institution than those who had no such record.[2]

The unmarried mother group known to private and public social agencies appears, therefore, to be made up of women

[1] Weidensall, " Mentality of the Unmarried Mother," *National Conference of Social Work 1917*, p. 287.

[2] Aronovici, *op. cit., passim.*

from the lower economic groups whose educational and occupational opportunities have been exceedingly limited. A disproportionate number of dull and feebleminded women are found in the group. A large proportion come from homes where relationships between parents were abnormal or where one or both parents were missing. The mental attitude and social background of the girl sex delinquent are also important in determining whether unmarried mother-hood follows sex delinquency.

Although family life was probably brought about more or less unconsciously as an attempt to solve that group of life problems associated with the perpetuation of the species, and society's treatment of the unmarried mother has not been to any considerable extent the outcome of rational considerations, there is evidence that in the face of serious problems of population growth, or the maintenance of numbers, society can so modify its policy as to safeguard its interest by protecting the lives of children of illegitimate birth. In a militaristic state or in times of war or when some calamity threatens the depletion of the population, value is placed on human life itself as a factor in maintaining the existence of the group and efforts are accordingly made to reduce the death rate of illegitimate children. Incidentally, improvement may be made in the condition of the unmarried mother by relieving her of some of the burden of the support of her child. It is recorded that the King of Denmark in 1707 alarmed over the depletion of the population in Iceland issued a proclamation ordering protection to the unmarried mothers of that island unless the number of children of such mothers should exceed six.[1] Frederick the Great, concerned over the loss of life due to the great number of

[1] Leffingwell, *Illegitimacy and the Influence of the Seasons upon Conduct* (New York, 1892).

infanticides during his reign and the resulting executions of the mothers, issued decrees forbidding employers and parents of pregnant unmarried girls to flog them, and such girls were instructed to report their condition to any married mother, who was ordered to assist them in every way possible. Further orders lessened the severity of the punishment of the unmarried mothers by the courts and every effort was made to secure such protection for them as would result in the saving of their lives and the safeguarding of their children.

At the end of the great World War the tremendous loss of life called attention to the necessity of lowering the death rate. As a part of the general policy various measures were taken to lower the abnormally high death rates among illegitimate children and to provide for their care. The Italian Commission for the Study of Measures Necessary for the Period of Transition from War to Peace specified that the work of assistance to mothers and children be extended equally to all and that " the old confusing, and obnoxious classifications between abandoned, mistreated, natural, legitimate, and adulterine children be abolished ". In February, 1919, the Provisional Assembly of Austria passed a law bringing under the supervision of the state all illegitimate children whether or not they were living with their natural guardians. Similar measures were prepared in Germany for the care of illegitimate children, of whom there were a million at the beginning of the war. Even in England where there had been no legislation of moment for more than forty years to change the position of the unmarried mother and her child, provisions were made for the extension of soldiers' allowances to mothers of their illegitimate children if paternity could be established.[2]

[1] Anthony, *op. cit.*, p. 84.

[2] *Illegitimacy as a Child Welfare Problem, op. cit.*, vol. i, p. 47.

Movements for securing the amelioration of the condition of the unmarried mother and her child have usually come about from concern for the life of the child, but in several European countries this movement to secure an improvement in the status of unmarried mothers has been a part of some general movement to secure recognition of women's civil and political rights.   The existence of a great number of unmarried mothers in the population at a time when women are giving attention to their own needs and problems will of necessity have some effect on the programs for reform which are proposed.   In Germany there was inaugurated in 1905 the Mutterschutz movement, later known as Die Neue Generation, which launched a program calling for new social customs relating to sex, new ethical ideals, and demands for legislative enactment.   This movement proceeded upon the fundamental assumption that some principle of applied evolution is the only ethical guide in matters of sex relationships and that changed conditions resulting in a large surplus of women, their employment in industry and the professions, and their advancement in education and experience demand radical steps of adjustment in the existing system of sex ethics.   The right of motherhood is asserted as one of the fundamental tenets of the Mutterschutz movement and "the eternal validity of monogamy" is questioned as a means of securing this for every woman.   Efforts to affect the standing of the unmarried mother in the community have caused the leaders of the movement to concentrate their attention on conventions which they regard as detrimental to the interests of women and to make efforts to insure that social legislation shall not discriminate between married and unmarried mothers in the aid and protection that it gives. As illustrative of the former they have tried to eliminate the term *Fraulein* as applied to adult women and the distinction which it makes in the two types of mothers, and the opportunity which it gives for social revenge and the persecution of the unmarried mother. The organization has kept the problem of the unmarried mother before the public and has been instrumental in securing the extension to them of the benefits of mothers' pensions.[1]

A somewhat similar movement was organized in England in 1918, the National Council for the Unmarried Mother and her Child.[2] This organization has endeavored to secure improvement in the legal status of the unmarried mother and her child, the right of legitimation by subsequent marriage, and more adequate laws for compelling the father to support his illegitimate child.   Other nations have had similar movements, and on the whole the tendency of the decade has been toward the amelioration of the condition of the unmarried mother by removal of those forms of discrimination which have forced women to assume an undue share of responsibility for the existence and the maintenance of illegitimate offspring.

A group of earnest interested women in Australia have united in the effort to secure support for a movement to secure the " right of motherhood " for unmarried women in a manner to attain eugenic ends and at the same time escape the stigma attaching to irregular sex relations. The plan is that by means of artificial impregnation by sperm cells obtained from men of ability and prominence whose wives are past the child-bearing stage, qualified spinsters of means and ability are to be allowed to attain to the dignity of motherhood without undergoing marriage or suffering disgrace. Unmarried women who desire to become mothers and who are adjudged fit for motherhood by the board of eugenics are to enter a " eugenic institute " where they are to remain

[1] Anthony, *op. cit.*, ch. iv.
[2] National Council for the Unmarried Mother and Her Child, London.

until after the birth of the child. They are then to be provided with certificates stating that they are " celibate eugenists mothers " and allowed to return to community life, presumably immune from social disapprobation. Records of the paternal kinship of the child are to be known only to the institute.

Summarizing, we may say that attitudes toward the unmarried mother have varied with the social and religious customs of the group and have been subject to social control in the face of social necessity. Between extremes where the mother is regarded as an outlaw and where responsibility for her care and protection is recognized in the interest of the state, there are types of treatment expressing every grade of social disapproval. The tendency for women of the past several decades to give careful consideration to their own problems and to claim a share in the making of laws which affect them particularly seems to be having its effect upon the whole group of problems associated with the relationships of the sexes by the demand that rational considerations form a larger part in the judgment of women who have departed from the accepted standards.

CHAPTER II

The Unmarried Negro Mother in New York City

HER BACKGROUND AND CHARACTERISTICS

WOMEN who have given birth to children out of wedlock and who, as a consequence of the difficulties arising out of the situation, make appeal to social agencies for assistance or advice constitute a group of the unadjusted or failures who are a direct cost to the community. They have violated the social code regulating the conditions under which children shall be conceived and born and have hampered themselves in the struggle for existence by a child which they are forbidden to desert and yet for whose existence and maintenance society has, in the ordinary course of events, made no provision. The usual difficulties encountered in the economic struggle are accentuated by disapprobation of friends and acquaintances who withhold their sympathy and coöperation. For women who are dependent upon their own efforts for a livelihood or for women whose parents withhold their accustomed support such difficulties are created that they are forced to appeal to specially constituted agencies for aid and for guidance in making their adjustments. An examination of the background and characteristics of such a group of women is a necessary desideratum before appraising the significance of the difficulties presented. Following is an analysis of the chief facts in the personal and environmental history of a group of unmarried Negro mothers who have at one time or another during the past five years come to the attention of the social agencies of New York City.

48

Birthplace.

Of the 500 records made use of in the study 447 stated the birthplace of the woman who was receiving the attention of the agency. Of these only 91 or 20 per cent were born in New York State; 45 per cent were born in southern states and in states other than New York State; and the remainder were foreign born.

TABLE No. 2

NEGRO UNMARRIED MOTHERS CLASSIFIED ACCORDING TO PLACE OF BIRTH

Birthplace	Number	Per cent
New York State	91	20.4
Southern States	158	35.3
Foreign Countries	155	34.7
Other States	43	9.6
Total	447	100.0

Of those born in New York State 80 per cent were born in New York City. The southern born included a majority from Virginia and the other border states with a smaller proportion from the states of the far South. "Other birthplace" included the states of the North and West. The foreign-born women were, with few exceptions, from the West Indies. Classification of the records of the separate agencies for the year 1920 show a similar distribution of colored cases with respect to the place of birth.

Comparison of the women chosen for study in our sample and the total Negro population of New York City for 1920 shows a somewhat different distribution as to place of birth.

TABLE No. 3

NEGRO POPULATION OF NEW YORK CITY IN 1920 ACCORDING TO PLACE OF BIRTH

Birthplace	Number	Per cent
New York State	39,233	25.7
Other States	78,242	51.3
Foreign Countries	30,436	20.0
Total	147,911	97.0

The foreign-born population contributed a higher percentage to the group of unmarried mothers included in our sample that might be expected from the proportion which they form of the total Negro population of the city; those born in other states slightly less than their proportionate number; and the New York born considerably less than the expected number.

A partial explanation of the greater proportion of unmarried mothers of foreign or of southern birth lies in the fact that these groups are made up of migrants with a large proportion of their women at the child-bearing age. The total Negro population of New York City shows the result of this large influx of migrants by a larger proportion of women within the child-bearing age than any other population class except the foreign born. This difference in age classes, however, may not yet be sufficient to account for the smaller proportion of the New York City Negro women who come to the attention of the social agencies because of the birth of a child out of wedlock. New York City Negro women have presumably been less subject to those conditions tending to produce illegitimacy than have the Negro women of the South who have come to the city. The former have had better educational opportunities; they have been less isolated from the thought and culture and social attitudes of other elements of the community; and, as a consequence, they find it less difficult to fit into the economic life of the community than do the recent migrants. It is also likely that they are more familiar with methods of contraception and abortion and that, in cases where birth takes place out of wedlock, adjustments are more easily made without appeal to social agencies than in the case of the woman migrant from the South or the West Indies who finds herself without friends in an unfamiliar environment.

In 1920 there were 30,436 foreign-born Negroes in New

York City constituting 20 per cent of the total Negro population of the City. This represents a considerable increase over 1910 when the foreign born constituted only 12.8 per cent of the total Negro population. Records of the year of entry of the foreign born into the country show the greater number to be recent arrivals, more than 30 per cent having come over in the years since 1916. Of the total number of foreign-born Negroes in the country in 1920 only 19.2 per cent had become naturalized citizens or had taken out first papers in contrast to 56.1 per cent of the foreign-born white population who had taken out first papers of citizenship or who had already become naturalized citizens. Recency of arrival seems to be a factor in determining the number and proportion of unmarried mothers who come to the attention of the social agencise since unfamiliarity with the environment and the difficulties encountered in the economic life result in problems for the unmarried mother which make an appeal to a social agency seem necessary.

Of the total number of foreign-born Negro unmarried mothers in our group 52 per cent had been in New York City less than three years; 25 per cent had been in New York from three to five years; and only 23 per cent had been in the city for a longer period than five years. Of the southern-born Negro unmarried mothers who were included in the study, 76 per cent had been in New York less than five years. Only 2 per cent of the total number of unmarried mothers included in the study had lived in the city less than nine months. Whether this smaller proportion of Negro unmarried mothers of longer residence in the city who came to the attention of social agencies represents a decrease in the illegitimacy rate with longer residence or only an ability to adjust to social conditions without the aid of social agencies, it is impossible to state.

AGE

Four hundred and forty-nine of the records stated the age of the women who were receiving the attention of the agency. These ranged from 12 to 41 years with an average age of 22 years at the time of the birth of the child.

TABLE No. 4

DISTRIBUTION OF NEGRO UNMARRIED MOTHERS ACCORDING TO
5 YEAR AGE PERIODS

Age	11–15	16–20	21–25	26–30	31–35	36–40	Over 40
Frequency	12	196	148	55	26	11	1

Twelve of the unmarried mothers were under 16 years of age, 196 were between 16 and 20 years, and only 38 of the 449 were over 30 years of age. Twenty-five and four-tenths per cent were under 19 years of age and 76 per cent were under 25 years of age. The age of greatest frequency was 21.

TABLE No. 5

AGE OF NEGRO UNMARRIED MOTHERS BY SINGLE YEARS

Age	12	13	14	15	16	17	18	19	20	21	22	23	24	25	26	27	28	29	30
Frequency	1	2	5	4	30	30	42	53	41	60	31	31	13	13	16	8	10	10	11

Age	31	32	33	34	35	36	37	38	39	40	41
Frequency	5	4	3	8	6	5	2	0	4	0	1

The foreign-born women had a higher average age than either those born in New York State, the southern born, or those born in other states. There was also a larger proportion of the foreign-born women in the later age-periods. The lowest average age was for those born in New York City.

Information regarding the ages of the white unmarried mothers of the city was not available for comparison. Studies of the Federal Children's Bureau, when both the white and the colored groups have been included, show that

Negro mothers of illegitimate children are on the whole younger than white mothers of illegitimate children but the colored group has a larger percentage 30 years of age and older than has the white group.[1] In Baltimore 26 per cent of the colored mothers of illegitimate children were 18 years of age or younger while only 13 per cent of the white mothers were 18 years of age or younger. On the other hand, 12 per cent of the colored mothers were 30 years of age or older while only 9 per cent of the white mothers were 30 years of age or older. This higher percentage of Negro unmarried mothers in the later age groups may have been due to the large number of West Indian mothers of illegitimate children in the later age groups.[2]

Facts with regard to age of unmarried mothers give grounds for inference as to causes of unconventional births. For women in the earlier age groups illegitimacy may be attributed to ignorance and inexperience, lack of acquaintance with group standards, and lack of knowledge of the penalties for violation of the standards. However when large numbers of mothers of illegitimate children are found in the later age groups illegitimacy can hardly be attributed to ignorance or lack of experience, but rather to lack of a vigorous public opinion enforcing group standards, or to lack of sensitiveness to such public opinion because of economic or other reasons, or to open defiance of the dictates of the group.

Not only are age and experience important considerations in causing illegitimacy, but the maturity of the mother at the time of the birth of her child is important in determining the nature of the situation presented, as is shown in cases 16 and 25.

[1] *Illegitimacy as a Child Welfare Problem, op. cit., passim,* pt. i; *Infant Mortality in Baltimore,* p. 157.

[2] *Infant Mortality in Baltimore, op. cit.,* p. 156.

Case 16.

Hester M.,[1] a colored girl 16½ years of age, was referred by a friend to the agency three months before the birth of her child. Hester's parents were dead and she had come to this country from Barbadoes three years previously with her aunt with whom she had lived. She had attended public school and had finished the sixth grade. Her aunt had been employed as a maid by a white family. She was accustomed to leaving home early in the morning and returning late in the evening. Her employers reported that she was a steady, capable servant, honest and reliable. The girl when not in school remained at home and was held responsible for keeping the room in order. The aunt took her meals at her place of work, the girl preparing her own at home. The aunt reported that after about a year the girl became " wild " and failed to attend school regularly. She began to invite boys to the room and stayed out late at night. She refused to obey her aunt about remaining at home. The aunt forbade the girl to run on the streets with fast girls and would not permit her to attend movies and parties.

A situation was found for the girl in the country where she " lived in " and did all the work for a small family. She had a well-lighted, comfortable room with bath. She did good work at first but after a few months she began to complain of the loneliness. She threatened to return to the city but her aunt persuaded her to remain. After a time she came to be on intimate terms with the ice man, with whom she went riding in the evenings. When she became pregnant he informed her that he was already married, his family consisting of a wife and three children, but that he was willing to do all he could to help her. Hester said that she had not known before that he was married but that he

---

[1] Names and initials used throughout the study are fictitious.

had never promised to marry her. She became negligent at her work, was dismissed, and returned to the city to be with her aunt. The aunt reported that she continued to invite men to her room and that when she remonstrated with her she left and went to live in a furnished room with another girl who, the aunt believed, was a prostitute.

The man responsible for the girl's pregnancy sent her $10 on two different occasions and then ceased to aid her. Her aunt refused to aid her unless she would return home and " settle down ". This she refused to do at first, but consented two months before the birth of her child. A baby girl was born at one of the city hospitals and the girl returned to be with her aunt for two months. A situation was found for her with a family in the country where she could keep her child with her.

Her employers reported at first that she neglected her baby and seemed to hate it. She began staying out at night and leaving the child alone. The baby did not grow and the girl angrily complained that it cried all the time. She complained of the loneliness; she said that she had too much to do, and that she had no time to care for the child. She was finally dismissed from her situation.

She returned to her girl friend in the city and again lived with her in a furnished room. The aunt reported that she was unable to do anything with her niece. The girl with whom she lived admitted that Hester neglected the child, which made itself a " nuisance " by crying all the time. Hester declared that she did not wish another situation; she said that she did not mean to " waste " her young life, but that she meant to have a good time while she was still young. The baby died at six months of age. Hester disappeared and her aunt knew nothing more of her whereabouts.

While the above is obviously a result of youth and inexperience and lack of wholesome opportunities for recreation, the following is a case in which a more mature woman who, while aware of the difficulties involved in her conduct, yet shows herself capable of meeting her own responsibilities in a thoroughly capable fashion.

Case 32.

A colored woman, age 30, light in color, neat and intelligent-looking, was referred to the agency for supervision by the maternity hospital where her child was born. The medical report showed her in good physical condition and, since she appeared intelligent, no mental test was given. The woman reported that she was born in Virginia but had been in New York ten years. She had gone two years to high school and had later worked as a seamstress in New York, earning about $15 per week. Besides the baby, which was three weeks old at the time she came to the agency, she had another child, a boy five years of age. At first she had said that she was a widow whose husband had been dead two years, but later she retracted her statement and admitted that the older child was also illegitimate. As his father she named a farmer in Virginia whom she said she had known since childhood. The man had come north to work for a while but had returned home when she had pressed him to fulfil his promise of marriage to her.

The father of the second child was a man whom she had met at a dance. He had told her at the time of their meeting that he was looking for a wife. He had promised marriage within a few days, but when he called upon the woman again he told her that he was already married, his family consisting of a wife and five children. Later when he was informed that the woman was pregnant he refused to be of any assistance to her. The woman was unwilling to bring suit against him in the courts for the support of her child because she dreaded the " fuss " and publicity and was afraid that her mother in Virginia would learn of the birth of the second child. She said that she would be ashamed for her mother to know that she had had a second illegitimate child.

When the social worker called on the woman in her home she appeared to be neat and capable. She had returned to her work but was now able to earn only about $10 a week because of the drain of the child on her time and energy. She was living with another woman who was also a seamstress. She reported that she expected to be able to manage without further help from the agency. The man had changed his mind about being willing to help and was paying the rent. Both of the children appeared to be healthy and well cared for.

MENTALITY

Only 66 of the 500 records made use of in the study were sufficiently complete to warrant classification as to the mental condition of the mother. The various social agencies whose records were used do not require a mental test as a part of the routine of examination and only in cases where the conduct of the woman led the social worker to suspect mental defect or abnormality was an examination requested. The number of occasions when such an examination was considered necessary, however, seemed remarkably small considering the close connection between illegitimacy and feeble-mindedness which has been claimed by some writers. Bingham found that 44 per cent of all those included in her study who had been illegitimately pregnant were mentally deficient.[1] Weidensall found only 20 per cent of the unmarried mothers included in her study to be of normal intelligence.[2]

[1] Bingham, *op. cit.*, p. 32.
[2] Weidensall, *op. cit.*, *passim*.

In almost all of our cases the mental examination took place after the birth of the child and during the time that the agency was endeavoring to find suitable employment for the mother. A succession of failures in positions found for the women by the agency or startlingly abnormal conduct on their part led to a request for a mental examination. Of those who were not examined it may be assumed that their conduct corresponded so nearly to what was regarded as the norm by the social worker that no inquiry into intelligence was deemed necessary. It can hardly be assumed, however, that normality of conduct or absence of unusual forms of behavior were always accompanied by normal intelligence. The greater number of unmarried mothers included in our study were derived from the group of domestic servants who ordinarily returned to similar situations after the birth of the child. They were, therefore, placed in situations to which they were already more or less accustomed; situations also in which no high degree of intelligence is required. Normal mental endowment might or might not prove a factor in the success of these women in household employments; for slight mental endowment coupled with a genial disposition might conceivably go as far in achieving success in such situations as a higher intelligence level coupled with a disposition to question the justice or expediency of the long hours of drudgery.

Of the 66 for whom data concerning the intelligence level were available, 51 of them or 78 per cent were rated as feebleminded or subnormal, 12 were of normal or dull normal intelligence, and 3 were sent to the psychopathic wards for observation and were later adjudged insane. As has been pointed out above, this sample of 66 can hardly be considered typical of the group of 500 included in the study, since only those obviously defective were singled out for examination. However, the need for a more extensive use of mental testing in the examination of cases is clearly demonstrated.

Of the 66 for whom the result of the intelligence tests were known, the employment records of 52 in the first position which they held after the birth of the child were given. With four exceptions, all were engaged in domestic service. One girl, who was a stenographer, returned to her position which she had held for five years previous to the birth of her child and which was held open for her during an absence of three months; two were factory girls who returned to their work; and one, who had worked as a seamstress, continued in her occupation. Of the 48 remaining who were found positions in domestic service, 31 were reported by their employers to be unsatisfactory in their work, that is, the employers were unwilling for them to continue; and 17 were reported to be satisfactory, that is, the employer was pleased for the time being and wished them to continue. In the group of 52, two-thirds were unsatisfactory and only about one-third satisfactory. The proportion satisfactory of those who were assumed by the workers to be of normal intelligence was slightly higher.

The following case illustrates the fact that adaptation to the situation presented by employment in domestic service may depend upon factors other than intelligence.

Case No. 52.

A colored girl, age 20, was sent to the agency for supervision by the maternity hospital where a baby boy had been born. The girl, light in color, neat and pleasant in appearance, had been employed at general housework. At the agency she stated that she had been born in New York City, her parents had died during her early infancy, and she had been brought up in an orphanage where she had had very good training in housework. The orphanage reported that her school record was poor but that she had shown herself docile and pleasant in disposition.   Upon leaving the orphanage a place had been found for her at general housework.   Her employers stated that she was not bright or quick but that she was a strong and capable worker, a satisfactory servant on the whole.   A mental test showed her to be of borderline intelligence.   The girl reported that at her place of employment she became intimate with the gardener, a white man, and continued the intimacy with him for over a year.   Up until that time, she said, she had seen little of men.   She was lonely and the man had been kind and had given her presents though he had never promised marriage.

When the man learned of her pregnancy he denied the intimacy and the case against him in court was lost.

After the birth of her child the girl was given another position at general housework and the child was placed in a boarding home.   The arrangement did not prove satisfactory to the mother, who objected to being separated from the child and spent a great deal of her time in going to see it. Another position was found for her where she could keep the child with her.   Here she proved a satisfactory worker and the child received good care.

She continued in her position for about two years, returning to the agency at the end of that time pregnant again by another white man who had delivered groceries in the place where she worked.   Help was given her until after the birth of the second child.   The case against the second man was also lost in the courts.

A position at general housework was again found for her. She took the older child with her and the younger child was placed in a boarding home.   The woman soon became discontented at work and insisted on having both children with her.   Her employers permitted this, but later complained that the woman became nervous and irritable because she was overworked. She was said to be in a continual fret about the children and her work and forgot to carry out orders which her employers gave. Her employers also complained that she was loose in her morals and kept company with the ice man and others who came to the house. The woman, when interviewed by the social worker, admitted that she had been promiscuous with men but stated that she now owned a doctor book which told her how to take care of herself and she expected no harm to befall her. Her employers reported that she had begun to neglect the children. The younger child fell ill and died. The mother was much grieved and reproached herself that it had not had proper food and care. Her employers reported that as her work and conduct improved after the death of the child, they were willing for her to continue in their service.

Five years after she first came to the attention of the agency the woman gave birth to a third illegitimate child. She was not certain about the father of the child so no case was brought in court. She was again given a place in domestic service, where she proved satisfactory. The older child was placed in a boarding home, the younger child remaining with the mother at work. The mother proved herself capable at her work and able to support the two children.

EDUCATION

Three hundred and seventy-eight or 75.6 per cent of the 500 records made use of in the study contained statements concerning the education and the formal school training of the mothers. The omission of this item in such a large number of cases at first appears inexplicable since the record of training and education would seem to be indispensable to the worker in giving vocational advice to women wishing to return to work. The omission, however, is probably less serious in the case of the colored girls than it would be in

the case of white girls, since the former are so largely confined to positions in domestic service where educational attainments and normal mental endowment are less important
considerations than energy and muscular strength and a willingness to submit cheerfully to the employer's regime.

The girl's statement regarding her schooling was usually
accepted as the basis for the record unless she laid claim to
unusual accomplishments or made statements which were
obviously untrue. In such cases an investigation was made,
if possible. It is to be expected that there would be a disposition on the part of the girls to exaggerate their attainments somewhat, and even if their statements were entirely
correct there is still much probability of error because of the
differences in the standards of the schools attended. A large
number of the girls came from the ungraded schools of the
South and the meaning of the term " grade " which was
used in the questioning was in many cases obviously not
clear to them. To the question of " grade finished ", the
reply was often " third reader ", " fourth reader ", etc.,
their advance in school being reckoned by the grade of read-
ing book which they were able to use regardless of whether
or not they had attained a corresponding proficiency in their
other studies. The worker who recorded such statements
had, in many cases, made an effort to evaluate the girl's
statement, and when such evaluations had been made they
were accepted at their face value in the study because of the
impossibility of interviewing the women or securing more
accurate information by any other means. Statements of
the foreign-born women were similarly evaluated but here
the number of ambiguities appeared to be less. The records
for those who had received their schooling in the North and
West, where educational opportunities have been better and
the system of grading more consistent, were more accurate.
" Grade finished " rather than " grade reached " formed the

basis of our tabulations; *e. g.* " fifth grade " should be taken to mean that the fifth grade was completed although the case may have gone several months in the sixth grade without completing the grade.

TABLE No. 6

EDUCATIONAL ATTAINMENT OF NEGRO UNMARRIED MOTHERS AS MEASURED BY GRADE FINISHED

Grade finished	Number	Per cent
None [1]	18	4.7
1		
2		
3	28	7.5
4	79	20.9
5	54	14.2
6	65	17.2
7	38	10.1
8	30	8.0
First year High School	21	5.6
Second year High School	10	2.6
Third year High School	6	1.6
Fourth year High School	2	.5
Normal or Industrial School	25	6.6
Business School	2	.5
Total	378	100.0

Four and seven-tenths per cent of the total number concerning whom educational data were available were illiterate, the percentage of illiteracy for our group being about twice that for the Negro population of New York City in 1920, which was 2.1 per cent. The average attainment for the group as a whole, leaving out of account those who attended business school, was 5.5 grades. This average is considerably higher than that for the women delinquents of New York State, which was 4.9 grades.[2] Thirty-three and one-

---

[1] Includes those who have never attended school as well as those who have attended but never finished the first grade.

[2] Fernald, *Women Delinquents of New York State,* Bureau of Social Hygiene (New York, 1920), ch. x.

tenth per cent of the women included in our groups had less than a fifth-grade education and 82 per cent had never attended high school. Eighteen per cent had some training beyond the grammar school.

The educational attainments of the women for the different population classes included in our study differs considerably from what one would expect to be the case from knowledge of their educational opportunities. Schools for Negroes in the South are notoriously poor and yet the average grade attainment for Negro women of southern birth was higher than for the women of any other population class. This apparent inconsistency may be explained by several considerations. Some of the women of southern birth had been in the city for several years and had attended the city schools. Moreover they averaged older than those of northern birth and their school days were more likely to have been completed. For those who had had their schooling in the South there was probably a larger degree of error in the records because of the ungraded condition of the southern schools and the further difficulty of checking up on the statements which were made by these women. Again, it seems reasonable that the average educational attainment of women migrating to the north would be higher than that of those remaining at home, and this fact might operate to raise the average attainment of our southern-born group to some extent. Furthermore it seems possible that those of the more recent immigrants from the South whose educational opportunities have been poorest have not come into contact with the agencies. The average attainment of the mothers born in New York City was lowest of all. This was due to the fact that such large numbers of these girls were in lower age-groups and their schooling was cut short by their maternity before the time when it would have been normally completed.

The percentage who reported attendance at high school, industrial school, and business school is unexpectedly high, 18 per cent. The majority of these schools were schools attended in the South and the probability of error in reporting is high. Many of the so-called high schools and industrial schools of the South are little more than grade schools with some high-school subjects and industrial training introduced in the upper grades. It seems reasonable to suppose that many of those who reported themselves as having done high-school or industrial work had attended these " high schools " and " industrial schools " for a few years without having actually done any of the high-school work. A smaller number had attended *bona fide* high schools; two were graduates of reputable industrial schools of the South; and two had had good business training.

Unmarried motherhood among the last-mentioned group occasioned less trouble to the agencies than those who had less earning capacity even though family relationships were more difficult to adjust.

Case 142.

Miriam M. was referred by the social service department of the hospital to the supervising agency for consultation and advice. The girl, 23 years of age, was born in Virginia, and had been in New York only six weeks. She was a graduate of a reputable normal and industrial school in the South. After graduation she had taught domestic science in a standard high school.

No mental test was given but the girl appeared intelligent and affable.

She had come of a good family. Her father was the superintendent of an orphanage and her mother, a high-school graduate, was his assistant. The brother of the girl was a medical student and the girl's elder sister was a high-school teacher.

The father of her child was a man about the girl's own age whom she had known since childhood. He had not promised marriage but the girl had assumed that an engagement had taken place. When he was informed of the girl's pregnancy he refused marriage, saying that he was too ambitious to cumber himself with the care of a family. At that time he left their home in Virginia and came to New York to enter business.

Miriam had been brought to the city by her sister who hoped to bring about a marriage or, failing that, to escape the disgrace of having the girl's condition discovered by friends at home. The sister who came with Miriam to the agency was a quiet, dignified woman of about 30 years of age. The girl and her family said that they were able and willing to meet all of her expenses.

An interview by the sister of the girl with the girl's lover failed to accomplish anything. The man reminded the girl that she was 23 years of age; that she had known what she was doing, and that he would accept no responsibility. He declared that he was interested in another girl who would mean more to his future than Miriam could. The girl and her sister were unwilling to bring suit in the courts because of the dread of exposure and disgrace.

The sister returned to her work in the South and the girl remained in the city with an aunt. On her visits to the hospital clinic she wore a wedding ring. She volunteered to the social worker the information that she felt the deception was justified since it would help to protect her family.

She became very devoted to her child. At first she planned to have him cared for in New York for a few years and then have him adopted by her family in Virginia. Later she reported that during her stay in New York she had become engaged to her cousin and would be married shortly. She planned to remain in New York and keep her child with her.

RELIGION

Only 291 of the 500 records stated the religion of the woman receiving the attention of the agency. Of these, 39 or 13 per cent were Catholic and the remainder were Protestant. Figures are not available which make it possible to state whether the percentage for the two groups are in excess of or below the percentage for these denominational groups in the general Negro population of the city. Within the Protestant group the women were divided into Protestant Episcopal, Methodist, and Baptist groups. The highest percentage of southern-born women and of those born in New York City were Methodists or Baptists; while a large number of those born in the North and West were Protestant Episcopals.

TABLE No. 7

BIRTHPLACE AND RELIGION OF NEGRO UNMARRIED MOTHERS

Religion	Birthplace				
	N.Y.State	British West Indies	Southern	Others	Total
Roman Catholic	5	17	15	2	39
Protestant Episcopal ...	15	51	7	13	86
Baptist	15	9	58	4	86
Methodist	17	20	38	5	80
Total					291

Religious ideas often affected the attitude of the woman toward her situation; and the religious ideas of parents and friends the adjustments which could be made.

Case 36.

Rosanna H. was sent to the agency for guidance by the social service department of the hospital where her child had been born. The girl, age 23, was born in Jamaica and had been in New York City three years She was a member of the Protestant Episcopal Church and a regular attendant. She had had three years of high-school work and had been a teacher in Jamaica. She had come to New York hoping to make an opportunity for herself to have lessons in singing. Unable to secure employment until her savings were used up, she finally secured a position at general housework. The girl was not strong physically and found the work very trying. She lived in cheap lodging houses because she was unable to afford better quarters. She stated that the man whose rooms adjoined hers offered to loan her money during the time she was out of employment. On one occasion she asserted that he forced himself into her room and that after that occasion she had continued on terms of intimacy with him for several months and that he had given her money and presents.

When the man learned that she was pregnant he wished to marry her but she refused. She said the man was of unsuitable ideals and low standards of life and that she did not wish to be associated with him. When she refused to marry him he called on her several times and was abusive. She wished the agency to assist her to secure another situation, away from the man where she would never see him again.

When the girl's child was born she wished to have him christened but was ashamed to take him to a clergyman because the fact of his illegitimacy would be revealed. She asked the social worker to make the necessary arrangements.

The girl was ashamed to write to her mother in Jamaica but a letter was finally despatched by the agency. The mother wrote refusing to have anything to do with her daughter since her disgrace. She spoke of the sacrifices she had made to give the girl cultural advantages and said that the girl had " thrown herself away ".

A place at general housework was found for her with a

family in the country where she could keep her child with her. Her employers reported that she was bright, capable and pleasant. Her child was well trained and well cared for, and on the advice of the social worker the mother started a savings account for him. It was reported by her employer that she had written again to her mother in Jamaica, asking that she be more lenient in her judgment of her. The mother responded that the girl had forgotten her God, her bringing up, and herself, and refused to be of any assistance to her.

OCCUPATION

In only 31 of the case records was there lacking information as to the occupational history of the woman who was receiving the attention of the agency. In some of these cases contact with the agency had been too brief for the record to be completed; in some cases statements had been made which were inconsistent or obviously untrue and attempts to gain the facts in the case had been unsuccessful; and in some cases the woman was already so well adjusted vocationally when she came to the attention of the agency after the birth of her child that a record of her occupational history was thought to be unnecessary. Of those concerning whom information was obtained 78.2 per cent had been gainfully employed in the year previous to the birth of the child and 21.8 per cent had not been so employed. Classification of occupation was made on the basis of the last position held before the birth of the child. The information given as a result of the classification can only be a rough approximation of the occupational status of the mothers concerned because of the failure of the records in most cases to name specific employments within the larger occupational groupings. Earnings were even less frequently noted in the records.

TABLE No. 8

OCCUPATIONAL STATUS OF NEGRO UNMARRIED MOTHERS

Occupation	Number	Per cent
Domestic and Personal Service	312	85.0
Manufacturing and Mechanical Industries	44	12.0
Professional Service	6	1.6
Clerical Occupations	5	1.4
Total	367	100.0

Mentioned specifically under domestic and personal service were chambermaids, child's nurses, cooks, elevator runners, lodging-house keepers, charwomen, waitresses, and workers at " general housework ". The largest number of domestic and personal service workers, nearly two-thirds of the total, were included in this last category of general housework. This seemed to indicate that in the majority of cases the women of our group were employed in families of the lowest economic group who employ domestic help at all, where only one maid is employed for the work of the household. In these cases the hours are usually long and the pay poor. Almost the entire group of those who were shown by the intelligence tests to be mentally deficient and who were gainfully employed were in the group of those doing general housework.

Manufacturing and mechanical industries included girls who were workers in factories and seamstresses at home. Factory workers included a larger proportion of those in the lower age groups than did domestic servants. More of the factory workers were also derived from the group of those born in the north and west. Domestic service included the highest percentage of southern-born and foreign-born women. There were six women in professional service, four school teachers, and two teachers of music. Those engaged in clerical occupations included three stenographers and two girls who had done clerical work in offices.

One hundred and two of our group were not gainfully employed in the year previous to the birth of the child. These included 58 housewives, 22 students,[1] and 22 women with no occupation.

"No occupation" included young girls who had not yet entered gainful employment but who were not in school, prostitutes, and those supported by men with whom they did not live or for whom they did not keep house. Housewives were those who had lived with the father of the child previous to its birth and were supported by him and also those who kept house for parents or relatives.

A larger proportion of our women (85 per cent) were employed in domestic and personal service than was true for the entire group of Negro women of the city gainfully employed in 1920 with a smaller per cent in manufacturing and mechanical industries, and a smaller proportion in clerical occupations and professional service. The distribution of the Negro women of New York City in occupational classes for 1920 is as follows:

TABLE No. 9

NEGRO FEMALES OVER 15 YEARS OF AGE IN SELECTED OCCUPATIONS
IN NEW YORK CITY, 1920

Occupation	Number	Per cent
Manufacturing and Mechanical Industries	9,131	22.4
Transportation	398	.9
Trade	321	.7
Clerical Occupations	745	1.8
Domestic and Personal Service	28,937	71.4
Public Service	27	.6
Professional Service	921	2.2
Total	40,480	100.0

Seventy-one and four-tenths per cent of the gainfully em-

[1] This group includes all girls who were in school at the beginning of pregnancy.

ployed Negro women in New York City in 1920 were in domestic and personal service in contrast to 22.6 per cent of the total number of employed women of all classes who were in domestic service.   Even the foreign-born women who rank next to the Negroes in the lowest-paid occupations had only 32 per cent of their number in domestic and personal service.

The above description of the characteristics of the unmarried Negro mothers indicates somewhat the nature of the difficulties to be encountered in the support of a child by a mother whose background is youth, ignorance, inexperience, poverty and, in some cases at least, mental incapacity and moral weakness.   The following chapter will deal more explicitly with the nature of the social situation presented by unmarried motherhood on the part of the group described above; the difficulties which have led to the necessity of intervention on the part of social agencies or to a direct appeal to the social agencies by the women concerned; the effect upon the woman's difficulties of her attitude toward her child and its father; the extent of her responsibilities; and the attitude of family and friends toward her and her child and their willingness to aid her or cooperate with her in meeting her difficulties.

CHAPTER III

The Social and Economic Difficulties of Unmarried Negro Mothers

UNMARRIED mothers are a burden to social agencies out of all proportion to the percent which they form of the total number of mothers who are dealt with by these agencies. In some cases they come to the agencies long before the birth of the child seeking advice in meeting difficulties which they are unable to meet alone or with the advice of family or friends; they come later for maternity care because of poverty at home or because of the fear of disgrace if the existence of the child is discovered; they come to seek financial aid in caring for the child or information about boarding homes for babies or institutions which offer more permanent care, so that the existence of the child will not be discovered or so that he will not be a handicap in seeking favorable conditions of employment; they come because they wish to discover the whereabouts of the lover who has disappeared and failed to fulfil his promises of marriage or financial aid; or because they wish advice as to means of forcing him to meet his obligations in the support of the child. Very frequently the difficulties are financial, incidental to the unaided support of a child under conditions of poverty by a young and inexperienced woman whose parents and relatives are unwilling to aid her in her difficulties. Occasionally no financial stringency has been experienced and the difficulty is emotional. The woman may have work, be able and willing to support her child, and yet be unable to adjust herself again to the situation after the birth of the child without consultation with some outside agency. Such a woman may need only advice and super-

vision during the period of readjustment. She has suffered
a shock, she has been terribly hurt by a new and unlooked-
for experience, and she wants to be reassured before going
on again.

We are unable to say to what extent the difficulties which
cause mothers of illegitimate children to come in such large
numbers to the attention of the agencies are due merely to
unmarried motherhood. We know that unmarried mothers
come to the social agencies for aid more frequently than do
married mothers; but we do not know whether they come
with greater frequency than do widows or married mothers
of the same economic and social standards whose children
have to be supported without aid from their fathers. The
reasons for the application of unmarried mothers to the
agencies are various and so complicated by poverty, ignorance, and other unfavorable elements in their surroundings
that it is impossible to state to what extent the difficulties
are due to the factor of illegitimate parenthood alone. The
immediate reasons for application to an agency as distin-
guished from the underlying causes do, however, throw some
light upon situations in which recourse to social agencies
has been necessary.

The reasons for application in the 404 cases where reason
for application was stated were as follows:

TABLE No. 10

CAUSES FOR APPLICATION TO SOCIAL AGENCIES BY UNMARRIED NEGRO
MOTHERS

Cause for Application	*Number*
Maternity care	204
Financial aid	48
Medical aid for child	41
Desire to dispose of child	20
Legal proceedings against father of child	33
Mother in court for other delinquency	58
Total	404

By far the largest number of cases come to the agency because of the need for maternity care. Eighty-eight per cent of the births in our study took place in hospitals or some other institution. The study of illegitimacy in Boston [1] showed that 77 per cent of the illegitimate births took place in hospitals while only 30 per cent of the total number of births took place in hospitals. In many cases this is due not only to the poverty and poor home conditions of the woman but the desire of the family to escape the gossip and criticism incidental to the birth of an illegitimate child in the home. Unmarried women applying for maternity care at hospitals are taken cognizance of by the social service departments and referred by them to agencies which are prepared to advise them concerning their social adjustments. It is by this means that some of the agencies receive the larger number of their cases. It is not true that all of the unmarried mothers under supervision by social agencies have come voluntarily for aid or advice or supervision. In fact a large number are " discovered " and referred by some other agency with whom they have come in contact in the course of securing medical or financial help. Unmarried mothers who have contact with the social service departments of hospitals are all from the clinics or the free or partly free ward service of the hospitals where women without means are given care. A woman who is able to engage a room or to pay for the better service at the hospital is not questioned as to her marital condition except in the matter of filling out the birth certificate of her child. Social service departments do not function for such women who are assumed to be capable of meeting their own problems, but for the women of the clinics and the free wards of the hospital who are not able to pay for their own care.

[1] *Illegitimacy as a Child Welfare Problem, op. cit.*, pt. ii, p. 102.

While many of the unmarried mothers who apply for free care state frankly that they are unmarried and base their claim for free care on the fact that they are without the support of a man, others are not so direct about the matter. Many attempts at deception are made, unmarried mothers reporting themselves as married or widowed or recently separated from their husbands in order to escape detection. By this means they hope to secure what the hospital may have to offer in the way of medical care and at the same time escape any attempt on the part of the social service department to advise, supervise, or reform them. Of the 50 cases of colored unmarried mothers coming to the attention of one social agency there were 8 attempts at deception as to marital condition.

Case 63.

Helen H., a pretty girl of 20, was received at the hospital a few hours before the birth of her child. She had been employed as a stenographer and had worked until the day before her child was born. She had avoided detection by lacing herself during the day and remaining in her room in the evenings. She was very light in color and was easily mistaken for white.

She at first reported that she was married and that she had recently separated from her husband. She gave her color as white.

Investigation of the home address revealed the fact that she lived in a colored section. Her landlady said that she had taken it for granted that the girl was colored and that she was not married. She said that the girl had been lonely and at times in such despair that she had threatened to take her own life.

The girl admitted that she had been guilty of prevarication, hoping to escape any attempts at supervision by social agencies. Inquiry into her parentage revealed the fact that she was an illegitimate child, her mother colored and her father a white man. The girl had been deserted by her mother when she was a young child and had been given to a foster mother, a distant relative of the girl's own mother. This woman had assumed responsibility for the girl's bringing up and for her the girl expressed a genuine devotion. She said that her foster mother had made many sacrifices in order to keep her in school. The girl had finished high school and had taken a course in stenography. She had found a good position and her employers had spoken of her as competent, efficient, and valuable to the firm.

Estrangement between the girl and her foster mother had taken place several years before. The girl said that her foster mother had refused to allow her any pleasures, had misunderstood her, and kept her closely at home. She had finally decided to break away from her home, secure a boarding place, and manage her own affairs. The foster mother said that the girl had been rebellious and guilty of prevarication in her dealings with her.

The father of the girl's child was a sailor whom she had met only three times. She reported that she and two other girls had gone riding with some sailors the third time they had met and were taken by the sailors to a " swell apartment house ". The girl had never seen the sailor again and did not know his name. She declared that this was her first and only sex experience. Her landlady and her foster mother confirmed her statement that she had not been " fast " with men.

The girl seemed to suffer keenly under her misfortune. She spoke bitterly of her mother's desertion of her and could not see how she owed anything to her infant since she had not wanted a child and his coming was only a misfortune to her. She said that she would not consider taking a position where she could keep her child with her.   However, she was unable to return to her business position at the end of two months and consented to keep the baby with her during the time that she was convalescing.   She had saved money sufficient for her expenses   She did not wish suggestions for her future unless her child could be taken from her and placed with an agency for adoption.

Upon her recovery the girl placed her baby in a boarding home and returned to her position.   Her employer, whom she had told of her misfortune, said that he " knew nothing of her private affairs, was sorry if she had been ill, and was glad to have her return to work."

The girl continued to pay the baby's board promptly and he was well supplied with clothes.   She visited him once a week to see that he received good care.   She declared, however, that she was not fond of the child and that as soon as possible she intended to arrange to have him adopted.

Forty-eight of the cases came to the attention of the agency by the application of the mother for financial aid in the care of an illegitimate child.   These cases were not greatly different from the cases of widows, who found difficulty in securing work and supporting children.   Cases of this nature had come to the attention of charity organizations, day nurseries and other philanthropic agencies.

Forty-one cases were referred to the agencies by milk stations, baby-welfare stations, clinics and other agencies having to do with the promotion of child health, and where the fact of a child's illegitimate birth had been discovered by accident.   These health agencies had felt the need of referring the mother to some other agency for aid or advice. One of the agencies received cases almost altogether from the courts where the mother had been brought for some delinquency or where she had come in order to institute bastardy proceedings against the father of her child.

MODE OF LIVING

The unmarried mother's home life during the year preceding the birth of her child and at the time she came to the agency was found to have much to do with the nature of the problem presented. If she was young and living with her parents it could be assumed that they would accept the major share of the responsibility for her care and subsequent direction. If she had been repudiated by her family, or if she was living at the home of her employer who accepted no responsibility for her care, or if she was living alone in a furnished room or in a boarding house, help by some social agency was imperative. Since our group was composed so largely of migrants from the South and West Indies, less reliance was placed upon family ties, since in many cases these had been broken by change of residence and many young girls were living independently.

Three hundred and eighty-five records contained statements concerning the home life of the mothers when they came to the attention of the agency. They were as follows:

TABLE No. 11

MODE OF LIVING OF UNMARRIED NEGRO MOTHERS AT THE TIME OF COMING TO THE ATTENTION OF SOCIAL AGENCIES

With parents	64
With relatives	37
With the man who was the father of the child	59
Furnished room	86
Board in families	47
At service	92
Total	385

Sixty-four of the girls were living with their parents during the year preceding the birth of the child and 37 were living with relatives, making a total of 101 who were living under the care of their families. Of the 64 who were living with their parents, 42 were born in New York State and the others had come from other sections of the United States to New York City with their parents. With three exceptions all of these were under 20 years of age at the time of coming to the attention of the agency. Fifteen of those living with relatives were under 20 years of age, the remainder being older women, more or less independent, who had maintained a residence in the home of a relative.

The attitude of these families is shown as follows: Ten of the families wished the girl to leave her home, and arrange to manage her own affairs without further cooperation from the family. In most of these cases shame at the girl's conduct and the disgrace which she had brought upon herself and the family seemed to be the chief reason for such an attitude; but, in some cases, the unwillingness of the family to assume further financial responsibilities was equally patent. In no case was the girl actually refused a shelter at home but in the cases mentioned it seemed to be understood that shelter was provided only temporarily and that other arrangements would have to be made as early as possible. In 18 of the cases the parents seemed willing to care for the mother but were unwilling to assume any responsibility for the child, wishing to have it placed with an agency for adoption or cared for permanently in an institution. In the remainder of the cases there was a willingness on the part of parents and relatives to aid the girl in caring for her child. In very few cases did this mean that the girl would be supported by her family and allowed to care for her child at home. In most cases the family or relatives of the girl were so situated financially that this was impossible. In the majority of these cases the girl went out to work again after the birth of her child but her family or relatives were willing to aid her in making her plans and be of all assistance possible. This does not mean there was on the part of these families any lack of shame at the fact of an illegitimate birth in the family. In some cases there was severe criticism of the girl for her conduct and resentment at the additional burden of the child's care. Homes in institutions for colored unmarried mothers and infants are more difficult to find than homes for whites and the pressure brought to bear upon the families to care for their unmarried mothers is probably stronger than in the case of white families.

In all but eight cases the families and relatives wished maternity care for the girl at the hospital. This was due in large part to the low economic level on which these families were maintained and the seriousness to the family budget of the expense of giving maternity care at home. In 35 cases the family was anxious for the girl and her child to receive care for a period of several months in a maternity home not only because of the expense involved in keeping the mother at home during the period when she would not earn but in order to avoid neighborhood gossip. In some cases parents offered to pay and did pay to have daughter and child cared for away from home during the first few months after the birth of the child.

Case 35.

Ethel M., a school girl of 17 years of age, was admitted to the free service wards of a maternity hospital a few hours before the birth of her child. She was accompanied by her mother, a woman of quiet, dignified appearance. She stated that her daughter was unmarried and gave her age and medical history. The New York address which she gave was found to be false; also the name which she gave was later admitted to have been a false one. Investigation showed that the family home was in New Jersey. The father of the girl was a prosperous business man who had known nothing of his daughter's condition.

The father of the girl's child was an unskilled laborer whom she had met by chance. She had been intimate with him only once and, while he was willing to marry her when he learned of her condition, the mother was unwilling for the marriage to take place, believing that the man was far beneath her daughter. The father was kept ignorant of the state of affairs, the mother fearing that she would be blamed for not having supervised the girl more carefully. She had hoped to send the baby to an institution for foundlings.

The child was stillborn and the girl's father was willing for her to return home. She did not return to school but kept books in her father's store.

A similar situation is shown in Case 231.

Case 231.

Ella E., a 17-year-old school girl, came to the hospital with her mother, asking for free care in the maternity wards. The girl was born in New York City and had attended public school regularly. She had finished the eighth grade.

The father of her child was a chauffeur, a man 24 years old, who had come to New York three years previously from Barbadoes and had boarded with the girl's family. The girl had been intimate with him over a period of two years. The man was willing to marry her but the mother would not permit the marriage to take place, saying that the man was the last person on earth whom she would permit her daughter to marry. The mother refused to have the girl's baby in her home though the girl returned there after leaving the hospital. The baby was left with the sister of the father and the girl went out to work again.

The man was ordered by the court to pay $4.50 per week toward the support of the baby. When the baby was ten months old, the girl married the father of her child. The mother refused to allow them to enter her home.

In 59 of the cases the girl was found living with a man, the father of the child, at the time of coming to the attention of the agency. The situation in these instances did not differ greatly from that of the normal family living in poverty which might be forced at one time or another to seek financial aid in order to keep itself together. It was impossible to judge of the stability of these relationships since in only a few instances did the records state how long the man and woman had lived together. There was one instance of a woman having lived with a man who was not her husband for 18 years and having borne him five children without any appeal for financial help except at the birth of the children, when the mother had had care in the free wards of a maternity hospital. Such evidence as could be found, however, seemed to indicate that the majority of these relationships were far less stable. Children of these unions were regarded in this study as illegitimate unless it was found that the parents regarded their union as a marriage.

Case 225.

Alice N., a woman of 34 years of age, came to the agency asking for help in securing free maternity care. She was born in Nevis, British West Indies. She had been in this country four years.

At the time of her application to the agency she was living with a man in a small crowded room which had no outside window. An oil lamp was kept burning all day. The woman had had three other illegitimate children by a different father. These children were living with her parents in Barbadoes. The man with whom the woman lived was a porter earning $18 per week. He had been a neighbor of her family in Nevis.

After the birth of the baby the woman returned to her

room.   The suggestion made by the social worker that a marriage be arranged met with no response at first, but there was later a consent to a marriage, which however did not take place.   The woman reported that the man was kind to her and to the child.   After a few months the family moved to better quarters.   The baby was registered at the Baby Health Station, where he was taken regularly by the mother for examination.   Both she and the man appeared to be much interested in the welfare of the child.

Very different was Case 255, where the girl had lived with a succession of different men.

Case 255.

Ora B., a colored girl, who had been living with a man in a furnished room, applied for maternity care a few weeks before the birth of her child.   She had worked at intervals in a factory during the preceding four years but when not working had always been supported by some man.   She had come from a large family in Virginia, and in order to escape the drudgery of farm life had come to New York at the age of 16.

During the time in New York she had undergone an abortion and had given birth to a stillborn child.

She stated that she could not remember a time when she had not had sexual relations with her own brothers, and she had had relations with a succession of men even before coming to New York.

A mental examination showed an intelligence slightly above normal.

The girl was well dressed and dignified in appearance at the time of her coming to the agency.   She talked well and seemed to have a good command of English though she had finished only the fifth grade.

Her record showed that she had been untruthful and untrustworthy with her employers, and on one occasion had been convicted of stealing clothing and jewelry.

After the birth of her child she returned to her family in Virginia for a few months, where she left the child with her mother, returning to New York again to live in a furnished room.

Forty-seven of the girls were boarding with families. This represents a situation somewhat better than that of the girls living in furnished rooms where there were few ties with friends or family relations. The girls who had no occupation and who were classed as " prostitutes " in the previous section were with few exceptions among those living in furnished rooms. The majority of these were in the age groups over twenty, women who were already committed to a life of delinquency and whose ties with family or friends were apparently of the slightest. This class of women was particularly difficult to deal with by the agencies. They moved frequently without giving notification of change of address; they were seldom at home when called upon, and they appeared irresponsible in their dealings with others.

Ninety-two girls were living at service in the homes of their employers at the time of coming to the attention of the agencies. The difficulties of life encountered by these girls were largely social, since their actual living conditions appeared in the majority of cases to be better than those of girls living at home or boarding in private families or living in furnished rooms. The life of servants " living in " is generally difficult and the hours of work are long. Agreements with regard to evenings off are not always scrupulously adhered to by housewives when the exigencies of family life seem to demand otherwise. Added to this there is usually little opportunity for social life for a colored girl

living at service. She of course may know the servant girl
of the family next door, but their " hours off " may not
synchronize and there is little opportunity for visiting.
Small wonder it is, particularly if she is young and still
eager for life, that she flirts with the iceman, the delivery
boy, or any of the tradesmen who come to the house, or
steals off at night for forbidden joy-rides or anything else
that offers diversion from the tedious drudgery of household work and the pettiness of her mistress. If she disap-
pears for a few days at a time and returns to work she may
find herself in as good standing as ever, since an irregular
life is not unexpected of one of her race and station.

THE UNMARRIED MOTHER AND THE FATHER OF HER CHILD

Statements of unmarried mothers to the agencies concerning their relationship to the fathers of their children
have needed to be considerably discounted. Aside from a
natural reticence in speaking of a relationship so personal,
there was an additional motive to misstatement or exaggera-
tion on the part of these mothers in the desire to secure some
kind of assistance in an actual emergency or in a continuous
economic condition with which they were unable to cope by
themselves. A woman who was continuing to live with the
man who was the father of the child often denied this, saying that she had been deserted and was in need of care; a
woman who was still receiving money from a man denied
this in order to secure further help; and many who knew
of the whereabouts of their lovers denied all such knowledge
because they were unwilling to start legal proceedings against
them. In practically all of our cases home visits were made
in an effort to verify the statements which were made to the
agency as to family status and need for help, and the conclusions contained in the records were the result of considerable investigation. In many cases the statements made by

the women were found to be substantially correct and their appeal for aid based upon a frank statement of the emergency in which they found themselves but the number of cases in which there had been misstatement and exaggerations fully justified the caution shown by the agencies in accepting the unverified statements of the girls. It is impossible to assert whether inaccuracies or misstatements were more frequent in the cases of unmarried mothers than in the case of other persons appealing to the agencies for aid.

The following classification of the relationship existing between the unmarried Negro mother and the man who was the father of her child is based upon the conclusions finally arrived at by the workers as a result of their investigation and which were used by the agency as the basis for dealing with the case in question:

TABLE No. 12

RELATIONSHIP OF THE UNMARRIED NEGRO MOTHER TO THE FATHER OF HER CHILD

Relationship	Number Cases
Common law wife	36
Paramour	81
Fiancée	88
Near relative	23
Lodger in same house	26
Employee	12
Chance acquaintance	144
Total	410

Common-law marriage has been used to designate the relationship which is temporary marriage in every sense except that of legal sanction. There were 36 cases in which the relationship was of this type where the man and woman had lived together for some time and had apparently accepted all the obligations arising from their relationship. The occasion of their appeal to the agencies was apparently no different from that which impels other families of the lower economic levels to seek aid, and appearances seemed to indicate that they needed only financial assistance to cope with the situation. No data were contained in the records which made it possible to compare the stability of this relationship with that of marriage more formally sanctioned, but of the 36 cases which were classed as common-law marriages the man and woman in 29 cases continued to live together after the birth of the child and the problem of the mother in caring for her child did not seem to be substantially different from that of the married mother similarly situated economically. Children of these unions were, however, classed as illegitimate unless the parents regarded their union as a marriage. The term paramour was used to designate the man and woman where there had been cohabitation for a more or less brief period of time but without any claim on the part of either party that the relationship was other than temporary or that a legal or common-law marriage existed. No satisfactory data were found as to the length of time which cohabitation continued, but the facts indicated that in only 23 of the 81 cases which were classed as paramours was the woman continuing to live with the man at the time she came to the attention of the agency, and in only 18 of these cases did the woman return to the man after the birth of her child. In 88 cases there had been a promise of marriage on the part of the man which had led the girl to enter into extra-marital sex relations, and upon pregnancy resulting, the man either refused outright to make good his promise or else informed the girl that he was already married and that other arrangements would have to be made. By far the larger number of cases were classed as the result of chance acquaintance in which there had been no promise of marriage on the part of the man; the relationship had not extended over any considerable period of time and the woman had not lived with the man or been supported by him although she may have received some financial help from him in the form of money or presents.

In some cases the mothers were asked the reason for entering into irregular sex relations which resulted in illegitimacy and the gist of their replies was entered in the records. Replies were not secured in a sufficiently large number of cases to warrant generalizations with regard to the group, nor is it possible to state to what extent the reasons given by unmarried mothers to representatives of the agencies are typical of their attitude toward irregular relationships. The following analysis is given, therefore, as typical only of what was contained in the case records concerning the women's statements as to their reasons for entering into extra-marital sex relations.

In eight of the cases of the more permanent relationships the man had been married and was unable to secure a divorce and this fact was alleged as the reason for the unconventional relationship. In one case where the man and woman had been living together for four years the woman stated at the time she appealed to the agency for maternity care that they had planned to be married after the birth of the child, seeing no reason why they should be married before. The record shows that a legal marriage did take place when the woman left the hospital after her child was born. In two cases the woman stated that the failure to have a marriage ceremony was due merely to " carelessness " and procrastination on the part of herself and her paramour. In one such case a marriage did take place during the time that the case was under the care of the agency. In three cases of common-law marriage the agencies were influential in bringing about a civil marriage.

Reasons for entering into the relationship in which the man and woman were designated by the term paramours were almost entirely lacking Careful study of the records show that in a majority of these cases the fact of living with a man for a short period of time was a mere incident in a long period of irregular relations. In three of these cases the woman alleged that she was without money or unable to support herself and had lived with the man in order to be supported by him.

Case 84.

Mary S., who was 21 years of age, had been in the United States only 14 months when she appealed to the hospital for maternity care. She was born in Jamaica; she was a Protestant in religion and she had finished the sixth grade at school. A mental examination showed her of average normal intelligence. She stated that upon coming to this country she had worked as a waitress in a hotel but being frail physically she had found the work very trying and efforts to secure more suitable work had not been successful. At her place of employment she became acquainted with one of the cooks, an American 23 years of age and a Catholic in religion. When the man had offered to take care of her so that she would not have to work she had gone with him to live in a furnished room. When she became pregnant the man offered to marry her but she refused because she had contracted a venereal disease from him. Because of this she was anxious to leave him. Friends aided her and she left him several months before the birth of her child. She admitted the birth of another illegitimate child in Jamaica three years before she came to the United States. She continued to appeal to the man for aid and he gave her small sums of money from time to time while she was attending a prenatal clinic and a clinic for the treatment of venereal diseases.

After the birth of her child her health continued to improve and a position was found for her at domestic service where she could keep the child with her. Her employers complained that she was dishonest and unreliable and accused her of stealing clothes and jewelry. The girl, when interviewed, complained of the difficulty of her work and the loneliness of her life. After a few months she left her position and refused to take another. Soon after she began living with another man, whom she told the social worker, she was unwilling to marry because of his excessive alcoholism. Another illegitimate child was born about one year later and the woman and both of her children continued living with the man, who continued to support them.

In the cases where the man had promised to marry the girl this promise was alleged as the reason for extra-marital relations, it being assumed that this was only preliminary to marriage. Marriage had been promised in the majority of cases before and in event of pregnancy. In nine of the cases marriage took place after the birth of the child and during the time that the mother was still under the care of the agency.

In 12 cases the father of the illegitimate child was a near relative of the mother. In four of these cases the girl's own father was the father of her child; in three cases the uncle; and in one case her brother was the father of the child. There was one case of a feebleminded woman of 32 years of age whose uncle was the father of her child, and one of a girl 20 years of age whose own father was the father of her child.

In two cases where the man had lodged in the same house with the woman, the woman asserted that she had not been able to pay her rent and the man had been of assistance to her. In one case the woman asserted that the man had at first entered her room and forced his attentions upon her, after which she had continued intimate with him over a considerable period of time.   In another case a young girl without previous sex experience asserted that she had been able to afford only the cheapest lodgings and that her sleeping room had been separated from that of the man by a curtain and that the man had entered her compartment at night.   In two cases of girls 14 and 15 years of age respectively the man had been a lodger in the house and had seduced the girl while the mother was out at work.

In 12 cases the man who was the father of the illegitimate child was the employer of the mother.   In four cases the father was a white man and in the remaining eight cases the employer was colored.   Ten of these cases were mature women who had evidently entered into the relationship willingly.   There was one case of a 16-year-old girl who was employed to care for the children of a neighbor while the latter was at work and who had been seduced by her employer's husband.   In another case an 18-year-old girl was employed by her sister to aid her in caring for a lodging house and the father of her child was her brother-in-law.

In the case of "chance acquaintances" reasons were given more frequently.   The majority of these girls were girls who were in domestic service and were living in the homes of their employers.   The most frequent excuse was loneliness.   Over and over again the statement was made that the girl was lonely and the man was kind to her, had taken her riding, or had given her presents or perhaps had only talked with her on the occasion of his visits to the house.   The fact that the girls so seldom had the opportunity to associate with persons of their own age and race must explain to a large extent their willingness to enter into irregular relations.   Some girls stated that they were afraid of losing the men unless they permitted sex relations; several girls stated that men were hard to get and keep.   One girl had entered into sex relations because she had been told by a friend that this would relieve painful menstruation, and another claimed that she had been advised to this step by a physician.

That an unwholesome social condition exists for Negro women growing out of the differences in the proportion of the two sexes in the total population is shown by the fact that in every census since 1890 there has been an excess of females over males.[1] This has not been true of the white population as a whole, nor even for the native white population. At the census of 1920 there were 99.2 males to every 100 females in the total Negro population of the United States. In New York City there were 90.3 males to every 100 females in the Negro population, which was an improvement over 1910 when there were only 85 males to every 100 females in the Negro population. This disproportion between the numbers of the two sexes lessens the chances of a large number of Negro women to be married; and this, coupled with the unfavorable economic and social conditions which confront them, probably increases their disposition to enter irregular relations. This hardship presses with greater weight upon the less well-to-do elements of the population since women of this class are under ordinary circumstances less sought after in marriage and more often sought for unsanctioned sex relations than are women of other classes.

MORAL CHARACTER OF NEGRO UNMARRIED MOTHERS

The term moral character used here has reference only to the mother's conduct with reference to matters of sex. Much of the material concerning previous moral character of the case is based on the girl's own statement since it was impossible to verify statements in most of the cases. In some cases where home visits were made the mother or

[1] Federal Cens··s 1920.

sister or some other relative of the girl contradicted the girl's statement regarding the description of her conduct, and these latter statements were also entered on the record.

TABLE No. 13

MORAL CHARACTER OF NEGRO UNMARRIED MOTHERS

Otherwise moral	160
Irregular	87
Promiscuous	61
Prostitute	11
Total	319

One hundred and sixty, or the largest number of cases, stated that they had never been immoral previous to their relations to the child's father and that all of their sex experience had been with one man. Eighty-seven stated that they had had relations with several men during a period of years but since they had confined their attentions to one man at a time they were classed as irregular. Sixty-one girls had been promiscuous, that is, they had relations indiscriminately with men, making no pretense of confining their favors to one lover for any period of time. However, as they had continued at work or had other sources of income than the occasional paltry presents given them by these men they were not classed as prostitutes. Eleven were prostitutes, that is, they were promiscuous in their relations with men and relied upon this as their means of livelihood.

A knowledge of the moral character of the unmarried mother is valuable to the agency in aiding her in her plans, not only in securing work but also in taking steps to establish the paternity of her child and in securing support from the father. The relation of the moral character of the woman to her attitude toward her child and her ability to care for him will be discussed in a later section.

Our study showed no correlation between intelligence and

morality. It will be remembered that mental tests were as a rule given only in those cases where some mental defect or aberration was suspected and that the apparently normal cases were seldom tested. Thirty per cent of those engaged in housework for whom moral character was indicated were classed as irregular or promiscuous, a larger percentage than for any other occupational group included in our study.

THE FATHERS OF ILLEGITIMATE CHILDREN

Information regarding the fathers of the illegitimate children whose mothers have been included in the study is very meager. In some cases where the acquaintance of the woman with the man was more or less casual she did not know his name, age, address, or similar facts regarding him. In some cases the man had disappeared and the woman so discounted what he had told her concerning himself that she was unwilling to report it to the social agency. In other cases the woman withheld information regarding the man in order to protect him from censure or blame or in the evident fear that action would be taken against him in the courts. The social workers who took the records were perhaps less assiduous in securing information concerning the father of the child because in many cases the confessed conduct of the mother precluded all hopes of establishing paternity or of compelling the man to contribute to the support of the child.

The marital condition of 231 of the fathers was as follows:

TABLE No. 14

MARITAL CONDITION OF FATHERS OF ILLEGITIMATE NEGRO CHILDREN

Marital Condition	Number
Single	153
Married	61
Widowed	8
Divorced	9
Total	231

In addition to the 61 married there were 8 single men who were living with a woman other than the one who had named him as the father of her child to the agency. These men evidently had obligations toward the women with whom they lived which prevented them from giving help to the women who had come to the agency for help. One man who was named as the father of the child of one of the women included in our study was found to be living with another woman to whom he was not married and by whom he had had three illegitimate children. Another man was named by two different " cases " as the father of their children, and this man reported that he was so involved with his landlady that he was able to marry neither of them. In 9 cases married men had deceived the woman as to their marital condition until after the woman had become pregnant and then had pleaded inability to be of service to her. The marital condition of the father was important in the consideration of the case by the agency, not only because of the possibility of arranging a marriage with the mother, but because the marital condition of the father and the number of legitimate children dependent upon him are taken into consideration by the judges of the courts in fixing the amount of support to be given by the father to the illegitimate child.

Information regarding the occupation and earning capacity of the fathers was also fragmentary. The largest number, 45, were indefinitely classed as " laborers "; 24 porters; 22 chauffeurs; 15 waiters; 8 truck drivers; 4 students; 4 barbers; 3 sailors; 2 bankers; 2 gardeners; 1 printer; and 1 actor.

The ages of the fathers ranged from 16 to the ripe old age of 72. The average age for the men was higher than that for the women; the average age for the men being 25½ years, and that for the women 22 years.

The attitude of the woman toward the man after the fact of pregnancy was discovered was recorded in a number of cases since this attitude was the important consideration in determining whether or not the woman would be willing to bring action against the man in the courts to compel him to support the child. In cases where the relationship was more or less permanent or where the woman was continuing to live with the man, the coming of a child was accepted as an incident in the relationship as in the case of married people. In cases where the woman had been promiscuous there seemed to be little feeling against the man except where the woman had made statements regarding her relationship to the man which were later proved to be false. The greatest amount of resentment was manifested by the girls who had been engaged to be married to the men in question and had been deserted when ever the fact of their pregnancy was discovered. In 30 out of 88 such cases the woman was willing to bring action in the courts to compel the man to contribute to the support of the child, a much higher percentage than for the groups where the relationship between the man and woman had been of a different nature. In many cases the attitude of the woman toward the man was such that in her mind his interests and his welfare were placed above that of herself and her child—as in case 77.

Case 77.

Mabel M., a colored girl 27 years of age, born in New York City, came to the attention of the agency through a prenatal clinic where she had registered four months before the birth of her child.

The girl had been a dipper of chocolates in a factory where she had earned about $9.00 per week. The girl's employment record showed her to be quick, intelligent, and

efficient at her work.   She said that she had been intimate
with only one man.   The man who was the father of her
child had had occasional engagements in vaudeville and the
girl gave his occupation as actor.   He was about 29 years
of age.   The girl did not know the extent of his earnings,
which were irregular.   They had been engaged to be married for several years but when the man learned that she
was pregnant he refused to marry her, saying that marriage
would be a handicap to him in his profession.   The girl
assented to this point of view; she said that she required
nothing of the man; and that she would not consider taking
action against him in the courts.

Her child died when he was three months old and her
fiance met the expenses of the funeral and burial.   After
this he wrote to the girl several times urging that they be
married.   The girl refused this, saying that she did not wish
him to be embarrassed on her account.   Finally she decided
not to see the man again.   A later record stated that she had
married another man, a chauffeur of her acquaintance.

NUMBER OF CHILDREN OF UNMARRIED NEGRO MOTHERS

One hundred and one of the 500 mothers who were included in our study had had one or more illegitimate children other than the one which was the occasion of their
coming to the attention of the agency.   In 399 cases, so far
as known, there had *not* been another child previous to coming to the agency.

The number of children born to each mother at the time
of coming to the attention of the agency is as follows:

TABLE No. 15

NUMBER OF CHILDREN OF NEGRO UNMARRIED MOTHERS

399 mothers had 1 child
60 mothers had 2 children
23 mothers had 3 children
7 mothers had 4 children
5 mothers had 5 children
2 mothers had 6 children
3 mothers had 7 children
1 mother had 8 children

In all there were records of 682 children having been born to the 500 mothers, about 20 per cent of the unmarried mothers having given birth to one or more illegitimate children previous to the one which was the occasion of having come to the attention of the agency. Some of the cases were followed for several years by the agencies and in addition to the 20 per cent who had given birth to an illegitimate child before coming to the attention of the agency five women gave birth to a second illegitimate child after coming to the attention of the agency, three women gave birth to two illegitimate children subsequent to their coming to the attention of the agency, and one woman gave birth to three other illegitimate children while she was under the care of the agency. The average number of children was slightly higher in the case of the southern-born and the foreign-born women than in the case of the women born in New York State or other northern states, but the difference was accounted for partly by the fact that the average age for the first two groups was slightly higher. The significance of the number of children per woman in making the adjustments to her changed economic and social status will be discussed in a later chapter.

The relation between the birth of a second or third illegitimate child and mental defect is apparent in the cases included in our study. Taking into consideration only the cases in which a mental examination was given, 30 per cent of those who were classed as feebleminded had given birth to a second illegitimate child while only 1.6 per cent of those who were normal had given birth to a second illegitimate child.

The difficulties encountered in dealing with a feebleminded mother are seen in case 50.

Case 50.

Jennie J., a colored girl of 25, was referred to the agency by the clinic of a maternity hospital where she had gone for prenatal treatment. She stated that she had been in New York three years; her birthplace was Maryland; her religion was Roman Catholic. She had been employed for short periods of time at housework but had never worked regularly. She admitted having given birth to two illegitimate children previously; she had also had one abortion, this being her fourth pregnancy. She was living with her mother at the time of her coming to the attention of the agency.

A mental examination showed the girl to be constitutionally inferior with a mental age of eight years, an intelligence quotient of 48. The girl's mother reported that at times she had been subject to convulsions, having at one period of her life had four or five a day.

Inquiry into parentage revealed the fact that the girl herself was illegitimate. Her mother was only 14 years of age when the girl was born, and she had later been confined in an insane asylum for a period of several years. At an early age the girl had come under the care of a charitable organization in the town in which she grew up and was placed for a period of time in an orphanage only to be returned to her mother again when the latter was released from an insane asylum. The girl stated that she had first been introduced to an immoral life by her mother, who had persuaded her to have relations with a white sailor when she was 15 years of age. The mother asserted that she had been told by a physician that such conduct would be beneficial to her daughter.

The girl had lived at intervals with two different men, one for a period of 18 months and one for a much shorter period. Her first two children died in early infancy, the last one, born while she was under the care of the agency, was committed to a foundling asylum.

After succeeding in having the third child committed to a foundling asylum the mother and daughter announced that they expected to return south and disappeared from the attention of the agency.

Only a very few of the unmarried mothers included in our study appeared to have arrived at any notion of prevention of conception by artificial means; and in the majority of cases where there was any expression of opinion, children seemed to be regarded as an inevitable accompaniment of an extra-marital sex life and their care was accepted as an onerous but unavoidable burden. In a few cases, however, a spirit of bitterness and rebellion at the heavy penalty which their ignorance had forced upon them was shown, as in case 21.

Case 21.

Carrie C., a colored girl of 26, came to the attention of the agency asking for care in the support of her four-months-old illegitimate baby. The woman gave her birthplace as South Carolina and her religion as Protestant. She had been in New York City seven months. The father of her child was a man of 55 years of age, married, and a laborer on a farm in South Carolina. The girl had finished the eighth grade at school and had taught in a country school in South Carolina. She had left home before the birth of her child and come to the city. Her mother had not known of her difficulties. After the birth of her baby she found a place for him to board and secured work in a factory. She complained of the laboriousness of her life and the difficulty she had in meeting all of her expenses since she was under obligations to send money to her mother in South Carolina as well as care for herself and her baby in New York. She complained bitterly of having to support the baby and tried to have him committed to an institution. She refused to consider taking a place at housework where she could keep her baby with her. To the social worker in charge of her case she appeared to have no concern for the child's welfare.

Failing to have the child committed to an institution she disappeared, deserting the baby at his place of board. No further word was heard from her and the child was committed to an institution.

CHAPTER IV

SOCIAL READJUSTMENTS OF THE UNMARRIED NEGRO MOTHER

IN 88 per cent of the cases included in our study the woman gave birth to her child in a hospital or other institution and it was therefore easy for the agency to follow her first steps at readjustment after her return to the community. In 36 cases mentioned where the woman was living with the man in a more or less permanent relationship, 29 of the births took place in the hospital and the woman returned to the man after leaving the hospital, presumably to be supported by him. In one case where the woman had lived with the man for a period of eight years and had been supported by him he refused to permit her to return home or contribute to her support again after the birth of the child. In one case the relationship had continued over a period of several years and the woman had given birth to five stillborn babies. The man with whom she lived had promised her that he would marry her if she gave birth to a living infant but failed to make good his promise in spite of the sixth child's good health. In 18 of the cases where the man and woman were paramours the woman returned to the man and was being supported in part by him at the time of the last entry on the record. In 49 cases the unmarried mothers married during the time that the agency was supervising their conduct. In 34 cases the marriage was to the man who was the father of the child, in 15 cases the marriage was to a man other than the father of the child. In 18 additional cases the woman began living with a man who was not the father of her child and to whom she was not married, and was being aided by him at the time of the last entry on the record of the agency. Where the woman was being supported by a man and was allowed to keep her child with her, her difficulties of adjustment were not economic; and her difficulties of a social nature were scantily noted in the records. In almost all the cases, however, the man furnished only partial support and the woman continued to go out to work during the day leaving her child with some one in the home. In many cases the woman was away during only a part of the day and was thus able to give some attention to the child. Adjustments occasioning considerable emotional stress and difficulty were encountered in the cases where the mother had married a man other than the father of her child, and in cases where the husband refused to permit her to have her child with her. In six of these cases the woman kept her child with her after her marriage, in two cases the child was left with relatives of the mother, in two cases he was taken into the home of his natural father, and in five cases he was maintained in a boarding home.

Case 58.

Theresa F., a colored girl 19 years of age, light in color and of a neat, attractive appearance, came to the agency asking for aid in the support of her two-months-old illegitimate infant. The girl stated that she was born in New York City and was Protestant in religion. She had finished the second year of high-school work; and had been employed for some time as a seamstress. She wished to find a position at general housework in the country where she could keep her child with her. A place was found for her by the agency and she did well at her work for a time, but after a period of several months decided that working with her child was too strenuous for her. The child was accordingly placed in a boarding home and the mother returned to her work as a seamstress in new surroundings.

The father of the child was a chauffeur, age 21, who had been engaged to the girl for over two years but had refused to marry her when he learned that she was pregnant. The case against him in court was won and he was ordered to pay $3.00 weekly to the support of the child, which he continued to do during the time that the case was being followed by the agency.

The girl continued her work as seamstress in another section of the city where she was able to earn about $20.00 weekly. At the end of a year she married a man who was not the father of her child, a well-to-do business man who was able to give her a good home. This man was not informed of the existence of the child whose board the girl continued to pay. After her marriage she continued to do sewing in order to meet the expenses of the baby's board, not letting her husband know of her work. The girl reported that she lived in a continual state of anxiety lest her husband should learn of the baby's existence and desert her. At the time of the last entry on the record the man had not been informed of the child's existence.

Owing to the fact that all of our records were of cases of recent date it was not possible to follow the woman's adjustment to the situation very far after her departure from the hospital, but in all but a very few cases a record was made of her initial steps at adjustment, which, after all, were perhaps most difficult for her to make. The most important step was the disposition of the child or the making of some arrangement whereby the mother could continue her work with the child. The following represents the manner in which the child was being cared for at the time of the last entry on the record:

TABLE No. 16

DISPOSITION OF THE CHILDREN OF NEGRO UNMARRIED MOTHERS

Place of Care of the Child	*No. cases*
At home with the mother	148
With relatives of the mother	90
With relatives of the father	12
With the mother at employment	62
At a boarding home	36
In a day nursery	6
In an orphanage or other institution	8
In the home of foster parents	9
Total	371

One hundred and forty-eight, or the by far largest group of
unmarried mothers, kept their children with them at home.
This includes the women who were living with a man and
were being supported by him; those who were being supported by a man but with a home separate from his; and
the few additional ones who were being supported or aided
by relatives or friends.   Only 103 of the women remained
in their homes all of the time and did not go out to work
during the day.   This number included the girls who had
returned to their parents or friends and were being supported
by them temporarily but who undoubtedly would return
to work after a short time, leaving the child to be cared for
by others; and the women who were living with men but
who were forced to contribute to their own support.   In 45
cases the girls returned to work soon after the birth of the
child, leaving the child to the care of friends or relatives at
home during the day, and returning home in the evening.
In many cases parents and friends were estranged from a
girl and refused their help because of her illegitimate child,
while in other cases friends and relatives who had not been
in touch with the girl previously, came forward and offered
their assistance when they learned of her difficulties.

In 90 cases the mother sent the child to be with her relatives while she returned to her work. This includes the cases where the girl did not live at the same place with her child, and where the entire responsibility for his care was assumed by some one else though the mother often contributed to his support financially. In 12 cases the child was taken by the father or his relatives who assumed the responsibility for his support. In two cases the mother died and the child was taken by the father into his own home; in two cases the child was adopted by relatives of the father; and in eight cases relatives of the father sided with the girl, and aided her in the care of the child.

Case 76.

Mary J., a colored girl 21 years of age, received maternity care in the free wards of the hospital. The girl had been in New York two years. She gave her birthplace as Florida. She had finished high school and had had some subsequent training in domestic science. In New York she had worked as a shopper and a draper, earning about $15.00 weekly. The father of her child was a cook, a man 37 years of age, whom she had known since childhood. He had promised marriage but when he learned of the girl's pregnancy he deserted her after first borrowing all her small savings. When the girl was ready to leave the hospital after the birth of her child, an aunt of the man appeared and offered to take the girl to her home. When the girl returned to work the aunt continued to care for the child. She reported to the agency that she was making every effort to locate the man, hoping to bring about a marriage. Failing this, she was willing to assume the responsibility for the child's support.

In 62 cases the mothers were caring for their children at their places of employment. Following the policy of keeping mother and child together whenever possible, and whenever this was desired by the mother, the agencies were able in some cases to find positions at domestic service where the mother was able to keep her child with her. Many of these positions were in the country in the vicinity of New York City and had, it was assumed, the advantage of removing the girls from the temptations of city life. The agencies which make a specialty of placing mothers with their babies have a selected clientele, women who are familiar with the work of the agency and sympathetic with its purposes. This appreciation of the work being done by the agencies together with the difficulty of securing servants for employment outside of the city, have caused women to be willing to offer a girl with an illegitimate child employment under very favorable conditions. Girls placed by the agencies are visited by them at their places of employment, and the agency being on friendly terms with both employer and employee has a good opportunity to observe the situation and, in some cases, to be of help in making adjustments. The results of this system of placing will be discussed in another section.

Thirty-six babies were placed in boarding homes while the mothers returned to their work. In these cases the mother was isolated from friends or relatives who would be able to care for her child while she was working, and she was not able or willing to take a place at domestic service and keep her child with her. In some cases it was manifestly unfair to urge this course upon the girl if she was physically unfitted to undertake the constant toil which such employment with her child would involve, or if she had had training and experience which would fit her for more remunerative employment. Six children were being cared for at day nurseries, the mothers coming for them in the evenings after leaving their work. In eight cases the child had been committed to an institution because of the mother's inability or unwillingness to care for it, and in nine cases the mother had permitted her child to be adopted. Separation of mother and child was resorted to only in extreme cases when no other arrangement appeared possible, as in Case 75, where a frail girl was unable to earn money sufficient to meet all of her obligations.

Case 75.

A colored girl, 20 years of age, came to the agency asking for aid in maintaining her illegitimate infant. The girl had come to this country three years previously from Barbadoes and had been employed at general housework. The father of her child, who had worked as a porter, had promised to marry her, but had afterwards claimed that he was not in a position to assume the responsibility for the support of a family, and so had failed to make good his promise.

The girl was not fond of her child and was unwilling to keep it and assume the responsibility for its support. She was anxious to give him away and appealed to several agencies for aid and advice. When it was suggested that she might be able to find a place at domestic service where she could keep her child with her and earn enough for its support, she refused to consider the proposition at all, saying that she was too tired and nervous and " wrought up " to work with the child. She had been unable to force the man to contribute anything to the child's support.

Investigation confirmed her statement that she had an invalid mother who was dependent upon her for support, and on whose behalf she had incurred heavy expenses for medical care. The girl's employers stated that she was reliable and prompt and a good worker.

The child was eventually committed to an institution, the mother pledging herself to contribute a small sum monthly to its support.

In 37 cases there was a record of the child's death in early infancy, and in these cases the mother returned to her employment and continued self-supporting. In other cases the records had failed to state what disposition had been made of the child after the first few weeks of its life. It seems reasonably safe to assume, however, that the children were kept by the mother or her relatives, since application for aid in the care of the infant would have been recorded.

It will thus be seen that in the vast majority of cases the responsibility for the care of the colored illegitimate infant was assumed by the mother or her relatives, and in very few cases was there a complete separation of mother and child by the commitment of the child to an institution. This fact among a group subsisting on the lowest economic level where the burden of child care falls heaviest, indicates the development of self-reliance and mutual aid to a very high level. This may be explained in part by the fact that agencies specializing in the care of colored dependents have not developed to the same high degree of efficiency as those for the white group, and the colored unmarried mother has thus come to rely on them to a less extent than has the white unmarried mother. The fact that institutional care is more difficult to secure in the case of colored unmarried mother and her child, and the fact that these must be cared for in the community, may have caused the development of a more rational spirit of tolerance and helpfulness in the situation than exists among other groups. The assumption cannot be made, however, that these conditions have operated so uniformly upon the racial group as to affect the thinking and attitude of Negroes toward the problems growing out of illegitimacy in any way which may be described as characteristically racial. Nor is there anything which would justify a different mode of treatment of Negro unmarried mothers upon the part of the social agencies of a community until the peculiar needs and problems of that community have been studied. Negroes form a peculiar economic and social, as well as racial, group, and for them the problems of dependency and delinquency are of the same nature as those for the other groups with their intensity increased somewhat by race prejudice.

PLACEMENT IN DOMESTIC SERVICE

Sixty-two of the women of our group or 16.7 per cent of the entire number concerning whom the facts were known after the birth of the child entered domestic service, " living in " at their place of employment and keeping the child with them. This movement is encouraged by the agencies because of a belief on their part that to keep mother and child together during the period of infancy encourages the growth of maternal love and that this regard for her child and the responsibility for its welfare serve as deterrents from future wrongdoing on the part of the mother. However, eight of the unmarried mothers who had been placed at domestic service by the agencies and whose records had been followed for a period of two years or more had, within that time either given birth to a second illegitimate child or had appealed to a prenatal clinic for medical care. It should be remembered that 85 per cent of our group were derived from those employed at domestic service, and that the hard and limiting conditions of that type of employment continue to operate after the girl has had her child and returned to work under the same conditions.

Social workers are not unaware of this fact but are limited in their ability to place unmarried mothers by the fact that they are so largely unskilled; that their experience has lain so largely in the field of domestic service; and that domestic service is almost the only occupation open to an unskilled girl where she can earn a maintenance for herself and at the same time keep her child with her. As has been stated above, the agencies usually make an effort to find places in the country where the girls are removed from their former associations and from the distractions of city life. Domestic service in the country seemed to appeal most to the girls who had met with criticism and rebuffs at home and were anxious to escape from their accustomed surroundings for a time. A few, too, who had tried placing the child in a boarding home and continuing their accustomed employment had found such a course expensive and unsatisfactory and had asked to be placed in domestic service with the privilege of keeping the child. One mother who had placed a child in a boarding home during the first five years of his life, came to the conclusion that the child was growing up to be spoiled and undisciplined. She therefore asked that a place at domestic service be given her near a good school where she could see to it personally that her child started off properly in his school work. No mother was recommended by the agency for employment in a home until she had first been given a thorough physical examination to determine her freedom from contagious diseases and her physical fitness for undertaking the work with her child.

In 46 cases the records concerning the girl's employment were sufficiently complete to determine the outcome of the experiment. In 21 cases the girl's adjustment to her first position where she kept her child with her was reported satisfactory to her employers. Those who were classed by the mental examinations as defectives were more frequently among the group of those who were unsatisfactory, but some of these girls appeared to be satisfactory servants. In very few cases did the records state the sort of domestic service to be performed by the woman; in the majority of cases where such a description was given the work seemed to be that of general housework for a small family where only one servant was employed. In a few cases the girls were employed as cooks only. There appeared to be no relation between morality and satisfactoriness as a servant, as large a percentage of those who had been promiscuous or irregular in their relations being satisfactory as of those who had been moral. An exception would need to be made where further immorality resulted in the birth of another illegitimate child, it being impossible in most cases to secure a position for a woman with two children.

In some cases employers stated why the girls were unsatisfactory and these reasons are classified as follows:

TABLE No. 17

REASONS FOR UNSATISFACTORINESS OF UNMARRIED NEGRO MOTHERS
IN DOMESTIC SERVICE

Reasons	*Number of cases*
Cruelty to child	3
Impertinence	9
Dishonesty	5
Laziness	4
Amentia	2
Total	23

Cruelty to child included cases where the mother neglected the child or refused to prepare proper food for him, and a case where the mother locked the child in a room and spent whole nights away from him while she sought distraction in some stolen adventure. The number of cases is too small to permit certain deduction. That the largest number complained of " impertinence " may possibly be more than fortuitous. If so, this might be correlated with the emotional stress which the mother is undergoing in the first months after the birth of her child and her separation from her accustomed surroundings. In five of these cases the relationship terminated by the girl disappearing with her child

and failing to report to the agency again.   One employer
reported that her maid was " as temperamental as a prima
donna "; and in another case the girl refused to get up until
after breakfast although she was supposed to prepare that
meal.

Among the 21 cases where the girl was satisfactory there
were included a larger per cent of the older women and also
a larger per cent of those who had given birth to a previous
illegitimate child but who had been able to make some
arrangement regarding the older child, keeping only the
younger one with her at service.

ATTITUDE OF THE UNMARRIED NEGRO MOTHER TOWARD HER CHILD

Much was contained in the records concerning the emotional attitude of the mother toward her child.   At best these
records were based upon the mother's statement concerning
her attitude toward her child.   In many cases the record was
based on the social worker's judgment of this attitude as
evidenced by the mother's interest in the welfare of her
child, her conduct toward him, and her eagerness to keep the
child under her care.   The attitude of the mother toward
her child was considered of first importance in dealing with
the case, and a summary of the results of these judgments
throws considerable light upon the attitudes which have
been influential in determining the policy of social agencies
toward unmarried mothers.   Since moral and religious attitudes are involved, the opinions of social workers and the
judgment which they have passed upon a particular case
would largely accord with the opinion of those supporting
their work and of the social class to which the social workers
themselves belong.   Unmarried mothers are likely to sense
this, and veer the expression of their opinion and attitudes
in the direction of what appears to be the prevailing mode

in thought and opinion among social workers. They do this in order to gain for themselves the minimum of criticism and opposition and to receive the maximum amount of help which the agency can afford them. The greater amount of dissimulation in the expression of attitude toward the child might therefore be expected to be in the direction of feigned love for the child since mother-love would be the approved and the expected reaction.

Society has in every stage of its development set its approval upon some type of motherhood and has tried by the conventionalizing of ideals to bring about the realization of the type. Perhaps the ideal of womanhood most widely adhered to in America at the present time is that of the " womanly " woman who finds her greatest happiness in motherhood and allied activities. A sublimated form of this ideal has been carried over into our conventionalized type of the unmarried mother. In fiction she has been the sentimentalized heroine, the woman " more sinned against than sinning "; " she who has loved not wisely but too well "; pitiful in her distressed and hopeless state, yet withal fond of her child and loving him, though she may do him harm in order to save herself. Tess, Lyndal, Hetty and other heroines of fiction may not in every case have cherished their children, but they loved them with that same intensity of maternal feeling which we have accorded to the conventionalized type of married mother. No other theme has received such constant attention from the Mary-worshipping artists of the Middle Ages to the latest portraits of the Negro mother and her child, as this theme of mother-love. Its effect upon the welfare of the offspring, and upon the continuance of the species is well known, but of the nature of this maternal love psychology has nothing very definite to tell us. Nurses and obstetricians, who have been in attendance at the maternity wards of hospitals, believe that there is an accentuation of the tender emotions of the mother toward the child soon after its birth, and that this is in some way connected with the functioning of the mammary glands. Some believe that the first tender emotions toward the child arise before its birth, and when the first movements of the foetal life are felt. After the birth of the child, and when the mammary glands have begun to function observers are well agreed that the mother in at least a large number of cases seems to have a passionate love for her child, and evinces a decided pleasure in having it with her. Her attitude toward her child may be very different from what she had supposed it would be, and a woman who has been very bitter about the coming of a child may become a devoted mother. This frequently happens in the case of an unmarried mother who has made frequent attempts to secure an abortion, and who has declared her hatred of the child, yet after its birth has become peculiarly attached to it, and made great sacrifices in order to avoid a separation. In other cases the attitude manifested toward the child persists after the birth, and the mother steadfastly refuses to have the child near her. In still other cases, of which hospital records show a considerable number, a mother who before her marriage had given birth to an illegitimate child which she hated and which she placed out for adoption without ever inquiring what disposition had been made of it, became again a mother after her marriage, and to the child born in wedlock manifested a decided attachment.

As to the nature of the emotion which is present at this time, Bain is quoted by McDougall [1] as saying that it is generated by the intense pleasure of contact with the young, though why this contact should be pleasurable he does not say. Watson is inclined to believe that this pleasure is derived from the stimulation of the nerves of sexual feeling

[1] McDougall, *Social Psychology* (Boston, 1912), p. 66 *et seq.*

in the mammary glands of the mother by the nursing of the child.[1] This might perhaps be met with the objection that the mother who does not nurse her child is as devoted as the mother who does; but even here the pleasure of all physical stimulation is not missing, and the love of such a mother may lack some of that element of passionate physical devotion which the nursing mother experiences. At any rate, social workers with many years of experience in dealing with the unmarried mother in her relationship to her child proceed on the hypothesis that if they can persuade the mother to nurse her child there is a much stronger probability of her becoming attached to it than is the case if she merely remains with it without nursing it.

Another factor entering into the love of the mother for her child is the tendency to identify herself with the being she has produced. "After all he is *my* child ", is a remark frequently heard from a mother who had arranged to give up her child and had then found herself unable to do so. This factor also explains the greater love of the married mother than of the unmarried mother for her child. The former has performed an act of which society and her friends approve; she is conscious of a virtuous performance, is pleased with herself, and her glow of self-satisfaction kindles into love for her child. So a mother who has not cared for her illegitimate child may become devoted to a child born to her in wedlock, as in the hospital cases mentioned above. This factor also explains to some extent the greater willingness of the unmarried Negro mothers to have their babies with them. The stigma of social disapproval does not fasten itself upon the Negro child born out of wedlock with such relentless cruelty as in the case of the white child, and the anguish of the mother regarding her

---

[1] Watson, *Psychology from the Standpoint of a Behaviorist* (Philadelphia, 1919), p. 258 *et seq.*

performance is not so great. This allows a more favorable opportunity for the intensity of the physiological love of the mother to come into play.

A further force inducing the manifestation of maternal love is the pressure brought to bear by society through the conventionalizing of the emotion which should be manifested toward the child. The woman in such a case must be gentle, tender, and womanly, and if she is married the husband must act the part of the " proud father ". No matter how unwelcome the event may have been to him, any deviation from the prescribed attitude is regarded as unnatural and meets with disapproval by neighbors and friends.

The ideal of the correct attitude toward the unmarried mother of a decade ago is shown in the following:

The chief object to be sought is her reclamation to good character and to good womanhood and so to strengthen and guard her as to prevent a recurrence of wrongdoing. *Incidentally* [1] it is proper to take into account her feeling as a mother and to shield her as far as may be properly done from the shame and disgrace to which she is exposed. There need be no scruple about creating an affection in the mother's heart which will increase the pain of parting. . . . The question arises is it right to free the young mother legally from the natural consequence of her error. Providence has ordained certain results which are intended to deter from immorality. . . . We have no right to deal harshly with those who are already under the Divine discipline, neither have we the right to interfere with the Creator's method of training and redeeming his erring children. Experience has proved that it is not difficult to obtain employment for a healthy young woman where she can maintain both herself and her child.[2]

[1] Italics not in original.

[2] " From the Illegitimate Child, Its Place in the Community," a paper read before the American Association for the Study of Prevention of Infant Mortality, Chicago, November 16, 1911 by Hastings H. Hart, Director Department of Child Helping, Russell Sage Foundation.

Of the 463 cases included in our study, where the infant survived the first four weeks, 437 of the records state the attitude of the mother toward her child. In 343 cases the mother was said to be fond of the child and devoted to its welfare; in 94 cases it was stated that she was not fond of the child, was indifferent to its welfare, and anxious to rid herself of the burden of its care.

Among the cases in which the mother was stated to be fond of her child were 28 cases in which the woman had been living with the man in a more or less permanent relationship, and 62 other cases in which the woman was living temporarily with a man, and was being supported altogether or in part by him. Here the economic handicap of the child's existence was less keenly felt and the maternal feeling could more easily come into play. It will be noted, also, that this group contained a large proportion of those of more mature age, and previous maternity experience, and this maturity of development physically and emotionally formed a better basis for the development of maternal love. Of the cases in which the man contributed to the support of the child, 76 per cent of the women were reported fond of the child. That this connection between financial aid and love for the child is not perfect is seen from the fact that 24 per cent of the mothers who received such support were reported to be not fond of their children.

Of the 94 cases in which the mother was not fond of her child, 62½ per cent were girls 18 years of age or under, girls who were immature physically and who were so handicapped by the existence of a child as to lead to a vigorous and decided effort to rid themselves of its care. There seemed to be some connection between the moral character of the mother and her attitude toward her child. Of those who had been promiscuous in their relation with men, 48 of the 61 were reported to be fond of the child, while of those who had earned a living by prostitution, 8 of the 11 included in the group were reported to be not fond of the child. Our data leads us to the suggestion that the attitude of the mother toward her child is correlated to a high degree with the hardship which she is forced to undergo as a result of the child's existence. This hardship is conditioned by her relationship to the man who is the father of her child, her own age and maturity, and the economic adjustments which it is possible for her to make.

CHAPTER V

Summary and Conclusions

THE preceding chapters have summarized the material given in 500 case records secured from New York social agencies which, in the course of other duties, render service to unmarried Negro mothers and their infants. We cannot say with certainty that the characteristics and the circumstances of the group which we have described were causative influences in producing illegitimacy since we have no means of knowing whether the conditions in question may not have been operative among other groups of women who have not given birth to children out of wedlock. Nor have we been able to say how illegitimacy among Negroes differs from illegitimacy among white groups because the comparative data necessary for such deductions was not available. The utmost accomplished therefore is a description of a deviating group without decision as to how the deviation was produced.

The group described in our 500 records was composed largely of young women who had come from an environment differing widely from that in which they found themselves in the City. More than one-third of the group were foreign-born. Almost all of the foreign-born were from the West Indies. An additional 35 per cent of the entire group had come to New York City from the southern states where the social system differs in many details from the complex city environment. It seems reasonable to suppose that this change from an early simple environment to an unfamiliar complex environment may have had some influence in causing ille-

gitimacy or, at any rate, have so multiplied the difficulties
of caring for an illegitimate child that an appeal to a social
agency was necessary.   A large percent of the unmarried
Negro mothers considered were in the lower age groups.
Twenty-five per cent of them were under 19 years of age and
76 per cent were under 25 years of age.   In a large number
of our cases therefore illegitimacy was accompanied by youth
and inexperience, a probable lack of acquaintance with group
standards and ignorance of the penalties following violation
of group standards of conduct.   The foreign-born unmarried mothers had a larger proportion in the later age groups
but this can be explained in part by the age composition of
the foreign-born Negro population of the City.   Age was
an important factor in the decision of the social agency as
to the disposition which should be made of the illegitimate
infant since women of more mature age were, unless feebleminded, more capable of providing care for their infants
than the younger members of the group.   Only 66 of our
500 cases had been given a mental examination.   Of these
three-fourths were adjudged of less than normal intelligence.
This sample of 66 cases cannot be regarded as representative
of the larger group since only those obviously defective were
singled out for examination.   There seemed to be some
correlation between intelligence and success in domestic employment though many of those regarded as mental defectives became satisfactory servants.   The percent illiterate of
our group (4.7 per cent) was about double the percent
illiterate for the entire Negro population of New York City
in 1920.   One third of the women whose educational attainments were given in the records had had less than a
fifth-grade education and 82 per cent had never attended
high school.   Comparisons of the different nativity groups
as to school accomplishments had little significance because
of the difference in the educational systems compared.

Thirteen per cent of the women whose religious affiliations were stated in the records were Catholic and the remainder were Protestant. Materials for comparison with the general population of the City as to religious affiliations were not available. The tenacity with which religious principles were held by the unmarried mother and her family seemed to influence the nature of the adjustments which she was able to make. Eighty-five per cent of the Negro unmarried mothers whose occupational history had been given had been engaged in domestic service previous to coming to the attention of the agency. Of all the Negro women employed in New York City in 1920 only 71 per cent were in domestic service. Other studies of illegitimacy with which comparisons were made revealed the fact that a disproportionate number of unmarried mothers had been derived from this occupational class.

Negro unmarried mothers under the care of social agencies are those who have not been able to make their adjustments unaided. Analysis of the reasons for which they came to social agencies reveals the nature of their difficulties. By far the largest number of cases, 50 per cent, came because of the need for maternity care. The fear of exposure and disgrace by the unmarried mothers and by their families and friends made the need of maternity care away from home seem necessary. Economic motives as well played their part here. The possibility of securing free medical service in hospitals probably added to the number of appeals for maternity care. A smaller proportion, 12 per cent, came for financial aid for the child; 11 per cent came for medical aid for the child; and 8 per cent came for advice about taking legal proceedings against the father of the child. In 58 cases the unmarried mother had been brought into court for forms of delinquency which had resulted in conflict with the law. Others had come with the hope of receiving institutional care for their children. Almost a third of the cases of which we had records were living with their parents or with relatives at the time of coming to the attention of the agency. Almost as large a proportion were living in the homes of their employers where they were engaged in domestic service. In 59 cases the woman was living with the man who was the father of her child. Thirty-four per cent were living independently in furnished rooms or were boarding with families. In the majority of the cases where the unmarried mothers were living at home the family or relatives were willing to befriend them and to give them assistance in caring for their infants. In many of these cases, however, much humiliation was apparently felt at the birth of an illegitimate child in the family. In cases where the unmarried mothers were living independently of their families it was imperative that the social agency give effectual aid in caring for the child or take legal proceedings against the father to compel him to contribute to the support of the child. The relationship of the unmarried mother to the father of her child also determined to a large extent the amount of aid which she would need. In 35 per cent of the cases the father of the child was a " chance acquaintance " of the mother and there had been no promise of marriage and no understanding that the relationship which resulted in illegitimacy was other than casual. In 21 per cent of the cases the mother had been promised marriage by the father of her child and this promise was alleged as the reason for the irregular relationship. In 81 cases the woman had lived with the man for a brief period of time and in 36 cases the relationship had assumed more or less permanent aspects. In 23 cases the father of the child was a near relative of the mother; in 26 cases a lodger in the same house; and in 12 cases the employer of the mother was the father of her child. In cases where an unmarried mother had been abandoned by the man and in cases where he had refused to contribute to her support the need for aid by the agency was more urgent. The feeling of resentment against the father of the child seemed to be most strongly manifested by the mothers in cases where there had been a promise of marriage which had not been fulfilled. Eleven of the women of the group were prostitutes; 61 admitted that they had been promiscuous in their relationships with men but without any commercial motive; 87 had had a series of lovers whose attentions had been received at different periods; and in 160 cases the girl had had sex relationships with only one man.

Little was known of the fathers of illegitimate children. Sixty-seven per cent of them were single and the remainder of them were married, widowed, or divorced. In only a very few cases was the occupation of the man given; the majority of these were in the class of unskilled laborers. The average age of the fathers of the illegitimate children was 25.5 years as compared with an average age of 22 years for the Negro unmarried mothers. Twenty per cent of the women in our study had had more than one illegitimate infant, the number of children per mother varying from 1 to 8.

The most difficult problem of adjustment for unmarried mothers was found to be the disposition of the child during the early years of its life since most of the women were under the necessity of continuing to earn. In two-thirds of the cases the child was kept by the mother at home or by her relatives when she went out to work. Sixteen per cent of the Negro unmarried mothers secured positions at domestic service where they could care for the child at the same time. In 12 cases the child was cared for by relatives of the father; in 9 cases the child was given a home by foster parents. In the remainder of the cases the child was cared for in a boarding home, day nursery, or other institution.

About one-half of the women who were placed in domestic service with the child were found to be satisfactory in their positions.

About four-fifths of the unmarried mothers whose attitude toward the child was ascertained were found to be fond of the child. A large proportion of the women of physical maturity and previous maternity experience were found in this group. The economic handicaps to which the mother was subjected as a result of the child's existence was thought to be a factor also in determining her attitude toward her child.

A previous chapter has revealed the fact that attitudes toward illegitimacy vary according to the customs and social conventions of the group. Unmarried mothers, as the more obvious parents of illegitimate children, have been the objects of the greater measure of social vengeance in the past. In the face of social necessity treatment of the unmarried mother may be subject to social control, and conduct toward her so modified as to protect her interests and safeguard the life of her child. We have seen Negro unmarried mothers confront some measure of social disapproval as a result of their unconventional behavior. In general they seem to use the same methods of meeting their difficulties as do white unmarried mothers of the same community—but, because of a lack of accurate information as to the social conduct of both groups it is impossible to state how closely Negroes adhere in attitude and behavior to the cultural pattern of the white elements of the community in the matter of illegitimacy. Some social workers believe, as a result of extended experience and observation that there is an increasing tendency on the part of Negroes to adhere more closely to the behavior patterns of the remainder of the community. And indeed, observation of the external phases of institutional or organized life of Negroes reveals decided similarity to the cultural pattern of the remainder of the community. In vain we look for and seek to isolate the trait " Negro " only to find ourselves confronted with the familiar traits of our own culture seemingly undifferentiated by any characteristic which we may call racial. There exist the same types of social organization, the church, the school, the secret societies, and the women's clubs with organization and duties similar to corresponding organizations among the white elements of the population. In Negro Harlem the same styles of dress are seen on the street; the same newspapers are read, and the moving picture shows and other forms of entertainment are not markedly different from those in any other section of the City. Not only does this outward conformity exist but there seems to be in the minds of the Negro people a passion for conformity, a refusal to admit or recognize differences setting them off from the remainder of the community. Even implications of physical differences are resented, as shown in the objection to the use of the terms " colored " or " Negro " and the resentment at the implication that the Negro is a member of a different sort of group. Bitter feeling is expressed toward whites " who never let me forget for a moment that I am a Negro " and this attitude extends to all efforts to call attention to differences between Negroes and other racial groups. Even statements made in public meetings with regard to differences in birth and death rates between white and Negro elements of the population arouse resentment because of the alleged effort to prove the difference or the inferiority of the Negro.

A further evidence of the passion for conformity to white standards and ideals is seen in the attempt of some Negro artists to approximate the physical ideal of the Caucasian race. Rene Maran, impervious to foreign influences, pictures his beautiful Negro woman as short, with broad swaying hips, large flat breasts, broad nose, large lips and characteristically Negroid features. American Negro artists with a few exceptions have painted their beautiful women with Caucasian features adding only the darkened pigmentation to give racial distinction and exotic charm.   True it is that this difference in physical ideal may be evidence only of the changed physical type in America with the increasing admixture of white blood but that this is not the sole cause is evidence from the phenomenal financial success of the discoverers and manufacturers of toilet preparations for Negro women designed to straighten the hair, lighten the complexion and give a glow of color to the cheeks.   Furthermore in fiction and in conversation the use of the descriptive term " brown " is coming more and more into vogue and the use of the term " black " discarded.   This effort of the Negro woman to conform in physical type to what is regarded as the ideal of feminine beauty of the group is not in itself an isolated phenomenon but is common to all women, whether white or colored; but it does reveal the fact that Negroes have not set up their own ideal of physical beauty but have accepted in many cases that of the white race.   Nor is this surprising when it is remembered that the success of the Negro in securing full rights to participation in the community life has depended so largely upon the closeness with which he has conformed to white standards both in type and in action.   Much stress has been laid upon the imitativeness of the Negro as a factor in his assimilation of American culture but perhaps more important in bringing this about has been the granting or the withholding of the goods of life in proportion as the Negro conformed or did not conform to the ideals of the ruling group.

Another example of the effort to approximate the white standard is the existence of a " color line within the color line " in Charleston and Washington and other centers where Negroes have long formed a considerable element of the population.   In these centers there exists and is recognized among the Negro element of the population an aristocracy of those who are light in color, who form an exclusive social set, who intermarry with each other, and who hold themselves somewhat aloof from the remainder of the community. Other reasons for social distinction exist however rather than the single one of lightness of color.   In many cases the members of these groups are descendants of ancestors who enjoyed freedom for several generations before the emancipation of the slaves and pride in ancestry as well as cultural achievement give reason for differentiation from the remainder of the community.   Because of their physical approximation to the approved type the members of the Negro groups of lighter color have been less generally excluded from the common life of the community from the days of slavery to the present time; they have been more successful in life; and are therefore an aristocracy of achievement as well as of birth.   Close association between the members of the group is encouraged by the fact that persons light in color can more frequently " pass " as whites at theaters, public gatherings, and even in business relations and they naturally choose as their companions those who enjoy with them these advantages.   Intermarriage of members of this group is due to the close association brought about by the factors just mentioned and also the desire to spare their children insofar as possible the disadvantages of racial discriminations.

Opposed to this passion for conformity in all aspects of conventionalized and institutional life there is evidence of a growing feeling of race consciousness on the part of Negroes, a desire to combat race prejudice growing out of evident differences in physical characteristics, and to gain by concerted action what individuals through their own efforts have not been able to secure.   Objects of concerted

action are the securing of rights to a fuller participation in
the life of the community and freedom from discriminations
on the grounds of race. Race consciousness then as a means
of obtaining these ends can be regarded only as a passing
phase in the development of Negro life, a temporary ex-
pedient to combat race discrimination. If race prejudice
should disappear the need for race consciousness as a basis
for cooperative action would have disappeared. As yet the
necessity for cooperative thought and action still exists and
race consciousness continues to develop with increasing intensity and, in some cases at least, excludes Negroes more
and more from association with other elements of the population. This growth of pride in race is seen from the increasing frequency of portrayal of the darker and more
Negroid types of beauty, the idealization of Africa as the
homeland, and the efforts to disseminate a knowledge and
appreciation of the art and civilization of the African peoples.
A pride of race is evident in the writings of some of the
younger group who exploit in realistic fashion and without
hint of apology the darker as well as the brighter shades of
the life of their people, glorying in their distinctive characteristics. Some of these writers lay claim to peculiar and
distinctive traits for their people, human characteristics
which the Negroes possess to a superlative degree. Among
these are mentioned his superior ability in music and art,
his unusual sense of rhythm, his irrepressible good-humor,
and his capacity for enjoying life under virtually any circumstances. Group consciousness is further manifested and
fostered by Negro newspapers of which there are more than
a dozen published in New York City alone. While city
newspapers are read for general news it is being more and
more fully recognized that news of especial interest to the
members of the race justify the existence of Negro newspapers and these are given generous support. Negro offi-

cials, policemen, librarians, and teachers are demanded more and more by the Negro community, which becomes sufficient unto itself, maintaining only economic relations with other groups.

For Negro women there exist the same problems of adjustment in family and occupational life which exist for women of other racial groups. These problems are intensified somewhat in the case of the Negro women by the factor of race prejudice. There is the problem of the choice between home and career for the increasingly large numbers of professional women; the problem of caring for the children of the woman of the lower classes who is engaged in industry and domestic service; the desire to enter new occupational fields in the face of discriminations based both upon sex and upon race; and the increased necessity for earning following from the low occupational status of large numbers of Negro men. Whether the economic independence of such large numbers of Negro married women represents merely a passing phase in the evolution of the form of their family life it is impossible to state but the trend seems to be in the direction of the woman devoting her entire attention to home activities as soon as the earnings of the husband are sufficient to permit this. Among Negroes at the present time there is evidence of a well-to-do cultured class with standards of family life characteristic of the Puritan era, intolerant of any departure from accepted standards. By this group the suggestion that Negroes might conceivably develop a system of sex morality and form of family life different from that of the other elements of the community is indignantly resented.

The traits of family life existing among Negroes at the present time show some variation from the family life characteristic of the remainder of the community. Marriages take place earlier, there is a larger number of women widowed, and fewer married women at the child-bearing

ages.   There are also higher illegitimacy rates among
Negroes than among any other population class.   However,
there is no conclusive evidence that Negro women are meeting their problems of family life in any way which may be
regarded as characteristically racial.   Illegitimacy rates
among the Negro servant class are high but we have no data
which make possible a comparison of the illegitimacy rate
among the white servant class in this country with the rate
for the Negro servant class.   However, illegitimacy rates
for white servants in certain European centers are much
higher than the corresponding rates for Negroes in this
country.[1]   In order to isolate differences in illegitimacy problems due to race we would need to compare the rates for
different racial groups under substantially the same conditions in this country and data for these comparisons are
not available.

[1] *Cf.* Mangold, *Children Born Out of Wedlock*, p. 76.

BIBLIOGRAPHY

Anthony, Katherine, *Feminism in Germany and Scandinavia* (New York, 1915); *Norway's Treatment of the Illegitimate Child* (New Republic, Aug. 21, 1915); *Public Opinion on the Subject of War Babies* (New Republic, May 8, 1915).

Aronovici, Carol, *Unmarried Girls with Sex Experience* (Philadelphia, Pa.); *Unpublished Study of Illegitimacy in Philadelphia.*

Bliss, W. D. P. (editor) *New Encyclopedia of Social Reform* (New York, 1908).

Boston Conference on Illegitimacy, Studies of 1914

Britannica Encyclopedia—article on " Illegitimacy."

Catholic Encyclopedia—article on " Illegitimacy."

Gallighan, Catherine, *Motherhood and Relationship of the Sexes* (New York, 1917).

Hart, H. H., *The Illegitimate Child.* *American Association for the Study and Prevention of Infant Mortality.* 1911.

Kammerer, P. G., *The Unmarried Mother* (Boston, 1918).

Leffingwell, Albert, *Illegitimacy* (London, 1892).

Lundberg, Emma O., *Illegitimacy in Europe as Affected by the War* (National Conference of Social Work, 1917).

Mangold, G. B., *Children Born Out of Wedlock* (University of Missouri, 1921).

Mayo–Smith, Richmond, *Statistics and Sociology* (New York. 1904).

National Council for the Unmarried Mother and Her Child. *Reports of* (London).

Newsholme, Arthur, *Elements of Vital Statistics* (London, 1899).

Nixon, J. W., " Some Factors Associated with the Illegitimate Birth Rate," *Journal of the Royal Statistical Society*, vol. 77, July, 1914.

Palzer, N. J., *Handbook of Information on Non-Support, Desertion and Illegitimacy* (Charity Organization Society, New York City).

Rowlands, E. B., " Legitimation by Subsequent Marriage," *Fortnightly Review*, vol. 107, March, 1917.

Smith, Mrs. E. L., " Unmarried Mothers," *Harpers Weekly*, vol. 58, Sept., 1913.

Smith, Rossie C., " The Love Child in Germany and Austria," *English Review*, vol. ii, June, 1912.

Social Hygiene, Journal of (New York City).

Townley–Fullam, C., " Moral and Social Aspects of Illegitimacy in Hungary," *The Forum*, vol. 50.

Trounstine, Helen S., *Illegitimacy in Cincinnati* (Helen S. Trounstine Foundation, 1919).

United States

Bureau of the Census. Birth Statistics. 1920.

Children's Bureau. Defective, Dependent, Delinquent Class Series.

no. 9. *Illegitimacy as a Child Welfare Problem.* Part I.

no. 10. *Illegitimacy as a Child Welfare Problem.* Part II.

Children's Bureau. Legal Series.

no. 1. *Norwegian Laws Concerning Illegitimate Children.*

no. 2. *Illegitimacy Laws of the United States and Certain Foreign Countries.* Ernst Freund.

Weidensall, Jean, *The Mentality of the Unmarried Mother* (National Conference of Social Work, 1917).

Werner, O. H., *The Unmarried Mother in German Literature* (New York, 1917).

Woods and Kennedy, *Young Working Girls* (New York, 1917).

Young, Alfred, *Catholic and Protestant Countries Compared* (New York, 1895).

INDEX